# CASE STUDIES IN
# CULTURAL ANTHROPOLOGY

GENERAL EDITORS

George and Louise Spindler

STANFORD UNIVERSITY

---

# THE KAGURU

*A Matrilineal People of East Africa*

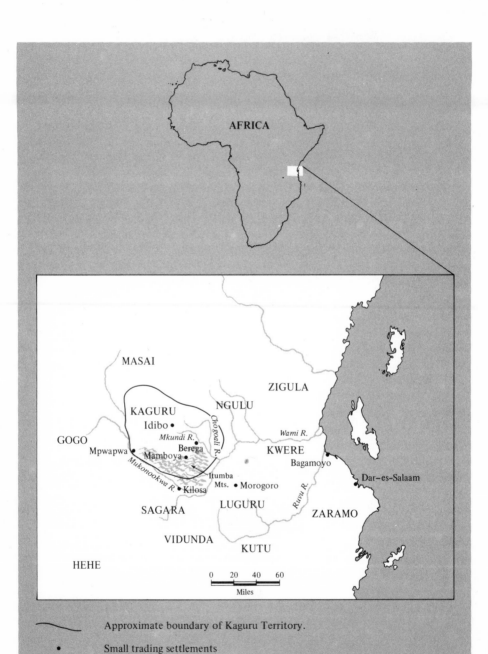

Approximate boundary of Kaguru Territory.

•     Small trading settlements

KAGURU     Large letters indicate tribe

Mamboya     Small letters indicate name of trading settlements

# THE KAGURU

## *A Matrilineal People of East Africa*

By

### T. O. BEIDELMAN
*New York University*

## HOLT, RINEHART AND WINSTON, INC.
NEW YORK    CHICAGO    SAN FRANCISCO    ATLANTA
DALLAS    MONTREAL    TORONTO    LONDON    SYDNEY

# TO KETTO

*Atanganye sana na jua, hujua!*

He who wanders much by day, he knows!

—Swahili proverb

Cover photo: *A Kaguru youth.*

Library of Congress Catalog Card Number: 71–144053
ISBN: 0–03–076765–2
Printed in the United States of America
89  059  9 8 7

# Foreword

## About the Series

These case studies in cultural anthropolgy are designed to bring to students, in beginning and intermediate courses in the social sciences, insights into the richness and complexity of human life as it is lived in different ways and in different places. They are written by men and women who have lived in the societies they write about and who are professionally trained as observers and interpreters of human behavior. The authors are also teachers, and in writing their books they have kept the students who will read them foremost in their minds. It is our belief that when an understanding of ways of life very different from one's own is gained, abstractions and generalizations about social structure, cultural values, subsistence techniques, and the other universal categories of human social behavior become meaningful.

## About the Author

T. O. Beidelman is Associate Professor of Anthropology at New York University. As an undergraduate, he studied social psychology at the University of Illinois. He did graduate studies in anthropology at the University of Illinois, the University of California, the University of Michigan, and Oxford University and received his doctorate in social anthropology from Oxford in 1961. He has done fieldwork among the Kaguru, Ngulu, and Baraguyu of Tanzania (1957–1958, 1961–1963, 1966, and 1967). He has taught social anthropology at Harvard University, Duke University, and Makerere University College, East Africa, and he was formerly a Fellow of the Center for Advanced Studies in the Behavioral Sciences at Stanford. He has published extensively on the Kaguru, Ngulu, and Baraguyu; he has also written on the Hindu caste system, the Nuer of the Sudan, and the Swazi of southern Africa, as well as on several East African peoples with whom he did limited fieldwork.

## About the Book

The author describes the Kaguru of east central Tanzania, East Africa, as a totality, but the description itself is highly particularistic. Indeed, as the author points out, the observation and analysis of the particular within the framework of the whole is the special strength of anthropology. Within this basic orientation land, livelihood, cosmology, clans, marriage, neighborhoods, life cycle, and the impact of the Christian mission are described and interpreted. A complex totality emerges as the particularistic details unfold.

The case study is also notable for the organization of observation and interpretation within a framework provided by the conceptual structure of anthropology itself as a discipline and as a body of theory. This helps the student to an explicit understanding of the nature of anthropology as well as to the nature of the Kaguru.

GEORGE AND LOUISE SPINDLER
*General Editors*

# Preface

In this study I describe the Kaguru, a people living in east central Tanzania, East Africa. Since some particulars of Kaguru ethnography are available in my published and forthcoming papers, I have concentrated upon the broader features of Kaguru society rather than upon details. I have, of course, provided some case histories and various other illustrations of what these social principles mean in terms of actual persons living according to such beliefs and rules. I hope to follow this more simplified study with more specialized monographs on various aspects of Kaguru society, especially political organization, initiation, folklore, and the relation of Christian missionary work to social change.

Much that is written for undergraduates studying social anthropology is so oversimplified that it presents an intellectually dull image of this discipline. In this study I have tried to avoid excessive use of technical terms and discussion of those minor issues which sometimes absorb specialists in a field; but I have also tried not to "write down" to students. I have attempted to relate the facts reported here to some of the more basic problems in social anthropology; without relating ethnography to social theory, social anthropology has little justification for being studied at all.

I first did fieldwork among the Kaguru for eighteen months in 1957–1958, when the area was part of Tanganyika, a United Nations Trust Territory with most of the attributes of a British colony. This initial research was through a grant by the Department of Sociology and Anthropology of the University of Illinois; in 1961–1963 I was able to do another eighteen months of fieldwork with the Kaguru and their neighbors, the Ngulu and Baraguyu, through a Ford Foundation postdoctoral fellowship sponsored by the Institute of Social Anthropology, University of Oxford. During that time, Tanganyika became an independent state within the British Commonwealth. In 1966 and 1967 I made two three-month visits to the Kaguru area through a National Science Foundation grant sponsored by Duke University and Harvard University. By then the Republic of Tanganyika had been reorganized and renamed the Republic of Tanzania. I have been able to collect and analyze further Kaguru data through additional research grants from Duke University and the National Institute of Mental Health. Unless otherwise stated, this account deals with conditions as they existed in 1957–1958. Since Tanganyika (Tanzania) achieved national independence in December 1961, radical political, social, and economic changes have been introduced. My account here cannot analyze these most recent changes.

My greatest debt in fieldwork is to the Kaguru and their neighbors, the Ngulu and Baraguyu; without their patience, kindness, and interest I should not have been able to live in their midst for so many months. I regard my stay with them as the most rewarding period in my life. I should particularly like to thank Miss Sandra Cohn, Professor John Middleton, and Dr. Rodney Needham for reading various drafts of this manuscript.

T. O. Beidelman

# Contents

Foreword   v

Preface   vii

Introduction   1

1. The Land and Its History   5

*The Broader Setting, 5*
*Kaguruland: Its Geography and Population, 6*
*History, 10*

2. Livelihood   15

*History, 15*
*Kaguru Economy: Agriculture, 16*
*Livestock, Crops, and Trade: The New Search for Cash, 20*

3. Cosmology: Man, Ghosts, God, and Order   30

*Cosmology and Society, 30*
*The Kaguru View of Space and History, 32*
*Clans and Ghosts, 33*
*Divination, 36*
*Witches, Sorcerers, and Magic, 37*
*Unusual Persons and Events, 39*
*Male and Female: Society and the Wilderness, 41*

4. Clans, Lineages, and Settlements   46

*The Nature of Social Organization: Kinship, 46*
*Kaguru Categories of Kin: Rules, Practices, and Social Change, 48*
*Tribal Members and Other Groups, 49*
*Kaguru Clans, 51*
*Matrilineages, 52*
*Settlements, 55*

5. Marriage, Kin, and Family   59

*The Strategy of Kaguru Marriage Arrangements, 60*
*The Form of Households, 67*
*The End of Marriage: Death and Divorce, 69*
*Children and Marriage, 70*

6. Neighborhoods and Chiefs: Political Affairs      80

*Defining Political Actions, 80*
*The Traditional Political System and Early Colonial Rule, 81*
*Recent Colonial Rule, 83*
*The Kaguru Native Authority, 85*
*Kaguru Court Cases, 89*
*Conclusions, 96*

7. The Person through Time      98

*Introduction, 98*
*Birth, 99*
*Initiation, 101*
*Boys' Initiation, 103*
*Girls' Initiation, 107*
*Rites of Marriage, 111*
*Burial and Funeral Rites, 114*

8. The Christian Mission: An Alien Institution Transplanted      117

*The Missionary Ethos and the Early Mission, 117*
*The Formal Structure of a Missionary Church, 119*
*Medical Services and the Mission, 119*
*The Educational Services, 120*
*Religious Services, 122*
*Recent Developments, 125*
*Conclusions: A Mission as a Social Type, 125*

Postscript      128

Glossary      131

References      132

Further Readings      133

# Introduction

THE AIM OF THIS STUDY is to describe an East African society in its general form. By this I mean that I do not emphasize any one institution such as kinship, economic organization, or religious behavior. Rather, I try to show how the division between these activities is mainly the artificial analytical device of social anthropologists. Any activity actually involves a wide range of meanings which merge. Thus, a marriage is an economic exchange of wealth for a woman who will be a source of labor and children; it marks the beginning of a domestic and familial group; it unites two groups of kin and therefore may have the implications of a political alliance; and the marriage is consecrated at a wedding by ritual with symbols which exemplify some of the deepest values of a society. It would be quite wrong to see marriage in terms of only one of these elements and not the others. It would be equally wrong to speak of the "institution of marriage" if by that expression we implied that marriage did not involve economic, political, and religious institutions as well. What we must do is to try to see social behavior within the framework of society as a whole, as, to quote Marcel Mauss (1954), "a total social phenomenon." Admittedly, this is a very difficult, perhaps even impossible, task; but it is precisely this commitment to an overall conception of a society that is the peculiar contribution of anthropology.[1]

How do a particular people define their proper relations with one another? What is it that defines a society? A society may be defined as a group of people who share values which they communicate with one another through commonly understood symbols, mainly language, but also gesture, art, music, and so forth. It is, of course, true that all members of a society may not hold identical views. For example, men and women tend to hold different views and valuations of certain activities and goals. The general idea of common values is, however, a helpful concept for us to use in trying to understand fairly simple, preliterate societies. Such values or symbols manifested in language define how a people incorporate experience of their physical and social worlds into some meaningful model for them-

---

[1] I try to discuss many of these general issues in a recent essay (Beidelman 1970a).

1

selves. Thus, it enables them in turn to know how to act to achieve their own particular goals and rewards. To the degree that this communication between persons succeeds, the members of a society are able to achieve most of their social ends—though always within the limits of the reasonable expectations one can have, given one's lot within a particular system. However, where we find serious differences in communicating and achieving these expectations, we find conflict, sometimes open violence, more often accusation, gossip, hidden betrayals, and other personal tensions, including, among the Kaguru, witchcraft accusations.

The ethnographer stands outside the society he studies so that his primary problem is to determine what the members of a society see as their goals. His first task, then, is learning the language of the society he wishes to study. By this I mean far more than simply learning a new grammar and vocabulary of words. He must learn and appreciate the ideas and values behind these words and must see how they form a system of beliefs, a model by which one gains a particular view of man, society, and the physical world. As I point out elsewhere (Beidelman 1970a), the anthropologist resembles a child in that he must also learn all the necessary ideas and rules by which an adult functions in his or her society. Like a child, he is first taught the ideal and proper scheme of things; then, as he gains in sophistication, as he matures within the society he is studying, he, like the sophisticated adult, begins to see how such ideas and rules may be used and even juggled for personal advantage or the advantage of one's group. One's conceptions of the ideal and proper take on the coloring of one's particular social position and problems.

In the first four chapters I present the basic features of the Kaguru environment, history, and social organization and the basic values and ideas which underpin that social organization. These ideas and values are existential. By this I mean that there is little about the "real" world (whatever that is) that necessitates one particular set of ideas or values rather than some other. Certain broad features of such idea systems may well be common to all societies, but clearly the particular details of thought, values, and symbolism within any particular society cannot be so explained. Furthermore, there is no reason to suppose that any particular set of ideas is the only or best system, given the facts of geography, demography, and technology of a society. Further, there is no reason to see a society as having a totally consistent system of ideas and values; indeed, we shall see that an entirely consistent system might well lack the flexibility required to operate within a real society. Anthropologists have always asked the question: To what extent is a system of indigenous ideas a consistent and useful model of a particular social reality? Anthropologists also want to know how social rules are consistent so that the various persons and groups which make up a society interact and reinforce one another's behavior without excessive conflict. Indeed, what would *excessive* conflict be? The belief that societies are, by definition, self-perpetuating and stable has mainly been developed through various theories sometimes labeled "functionalism." Such theories assume that social values and rules form systems which are fairly constant and enduring and that if change occurs, it derives from the intrusion of forces originally outside the society. The values of such a theory are obvious, for it predisposes the researcher to find a common meaning and interdependence between all the features of a society. There has long been an assumption that if some custom exists within a society, it must exist because it contributes to the ongoing qualities of that society. This could, of course, lead to many unwarranted explanations about social facts; nonetheless, such an assumption does sensitize fieldworkers to observe a wide range of facts and to try to find meanings even in those which at first may appear to be simply inexplicable customs. If we remember how most fieldworkers learn about a society, we can also see why there is some predisposition toward describing societies as perhaps even more consistent, homogeneous, and idealized than they actually are. Edmund Leach (1954: "Introduction") has sharply criticized this trend.

Such functionalist theories sometimes blind fieldworkers as to how societies change. Surely, one would not say that societies only change due to forces from outside. Invention and revolution and creativity are also important forces *within* societies.

We have all read the standard descriptive ethnographies with their emphases upon social organization, norms, and customs. In many of these studies a discussion of religious practices and beliefs is simply tacked on, often with little attempt by the author to relate this aspect of life to the other sectors of the society. Perhaps in part this is due to our own bias derived from our society in which religion is often simply defined as something one does in church. I have tried to show in Chapter 3 how certain basic notions underlie Kaguru society. These would ordinarily fall under the label of "religious beliefs," and I present them at the beginning of this study since these ideas and values must be understood if we are to see the other rules of Kaguru social behavior for what they are —the rational outcome of a basic world view of man and society and their relation to the physical world. In Chapter 7 I try to show how these values are repeatedly utilized within Kaguru society to weld together various groups. Through various types of ritual Kaguru are made intensely aware of and are able to express symbolically those affective or emotional states related to such values.

Prior to my fieldwork with the Kaguru, no dependable ethnographic material had been published on this society, and little of value had been written about their neighbors. There is still no comprehensive study published for any matrilineal society in this part of Africa. I have already published a fair number of papers on the Kaguru and their neighbors covering various details of their culture, from ironworking and botanical terminology to kinship, folklore, and colonial administration. The task remains only half completed. However, a more general study, tying these disparate elements into a more meaningful whole, may allow both students and colleagues to comprehend Kaguru society somewhat better, at least until a more detailed and specialized monograph is completed. Although this book is written primarily to be read by students, I hope it may also be of some interest to my professional colleagues. I have tried to write for both groups since I believe that if anthropology has any useful theory, this should be formulated in a manner which is understandable to all levels of persons interested in social studies. When it is not, we may well wonder whether jargon is not serving to mask unclear thought.

# 1

# The Land and Its History

## The Broader Setting

THE KAGURU LIVE in eastcentral Tanzania (formerly Tanganyika) about 160 miles inland from the capital, Dar es Salaam. Kaguru claim a land, Ukaguru, which is roughly about 3600 square miles in extent. However, much of the outer fringes of this land is claimed by neighboring peoples who, along with many migrant laborers working on estates in the eastern border areas, now live side by side with Kaguru. Ukaguru proper, the center of the Kaguru homeland, has an area of about 2000 square miles; this area is inhabited mainly by Kaguru, and it is to this area that most of this study applies. Today the Kaguru probably number considerably more than 100,000. In 1957, when I first worked in Kaguruland, a government census recorded 87,000 Kaguru. Unlike many other peoples in East Africa, the overwhelming majority of Kaguru live within their own homeland. Very few have sought work elsewhere.

The Kaguru are the most westward of a cluster of culturally similar peoples in eastern Tanzania, a cluster distinguished by closely related Bantu languages, similar economies, customs, traditions, and, above all, social organization based on matrilineal succession, that is, descent through women.[1] The other peoples in this cluster are the Luguru, Sagara, Ngulu, Vidunda, Kutu, Zaramo, and Zigula. All of the peoples neighboring this cultural cluster order their societies by descent through men and have quite different customs and traditions. Kaguru are very aware of these differences and sometimes try to account for their similarity to their eastern neighbors by suggesting a possible common origin. In general, Kaguru speak very disparagingly about neighboring cultures, though far less so of their matrilineal neighbors than, say, of the Masai-type peoples to the north, who used to raid them, or of the Gogo to the west, who, due to frequent famines, often become vulnerable refugees in Kaguruland. Even in the past, Kaguruland, due to its location between very different ecological zones, was the center of considerable

---

[1] I discuss these common features elsewhere (Beidelman 1967: xi–xiv).

contact between various disparate peoples. Today fairly large colonies of non-Kaguru may be found in Kaguruland proper, and even the earliest historical accounts in the 1880s remark upon the presence of such alien groups. As a consequence, most Kaguru are quite aware of many possible alternatives to their own culture, and many are polylingual, so that the fieldworker is confronted often with informants with a high degree of sophistication in terms of their awareness of cultural relativism. Although the terrain and climate within this area vary considerably, Kaguruland appears as a distinct geographical entity when it is contrasted with much of the land which surrounds it.

## Kaguruland: Its Geography and Population

The mountains of Kaguruland form part of a roughly defined belt of mountains and hills extending diagonally from southwest to northeast across the length of Tanzania. This belt divides the narrow coastal lowlands from the vast central plateau which comprises two-thirds of Tanzania. To the east of the mountains, toward the coast, are the lowlands, which are not very favorable for African cultivation or cattle-keeping and which afforded little natural protection from the African and Arab raiders who disturbed much of Tanzania in the nineteenth century. To the west and north of this mountainous belt is the great central plateau, a high rolling plain of rough grassland and thornscrub frequently broken by low hills. This is suited to a pastoral economy but is less favorable for agriculture due to the undependability of the rains. The portion of the plateau adjoining the mountain belt near Kaguruland is the poorest and least populated area of Tanzania, forming the Masai Steppe to the north and Ugogo to the west, inhabited by Masai and Gogo, respectively.

The mountain belt is divided into a number of discrete highlands separated from one another by the various river valleys cutting through this belt on their way to the Indian Ocean. The part of this belt known as Kaguruland is marked off on both the north and south by various river systems. To the south the Mukondokwa River Valley and associated wet season swamps divide Kaguruland from the lands of the Sagara, Vidunda, and Luguru, other matrilineal peoples fairly similar to the Kaguru. To the northeast the Mkundi and Chogoali rivers divide Kaguruland from the Ngulu, another hill people who very closely resemble the Kaguru and who occupy a mountain-hill-lowland ecological complex quite similar, though smaller, to Kaguruland.

If we wish to understand the political and economic relations between the people of Kaguruland and their neighbors, and the past importance of Kaguruland in Arab and European trade and politics, then we must keep in mind the contrast between the mountain belt and the adjoining central plateau to the west and coastal lowlands to the east. Compared to these areas, mountain areas such as Kaguruland were more healthful, regularly supplied with water, and more defensible and afforded more dependable conditions for agriculture and livestock husbandry. The overoptimistic interest which early German colonizers and British missionaries took in this area was important to its development. The enthusiasm of these early European adventurers can only be understood if we keep Kaguruland's location in mind. Early British missionaries compared the area to the Scottish highlands, and Sir Henry Stanley (vol. 1, 1899:72–73), en route to search for Livingstone, praised Kaguruland, which he compared to the beauties of the Allegheny Mountains—curious tributes confusing beauty with habitability since both these areas remain pockets of poverty in Europe and America.

Kaguruland may be divided into three geographic areas: lowlands, mountains, and plateau:

1. LOWLANDS.   All of this area lies below 2000 feet altitude and is entirely in the eastern part of Kaguruland, less than 19 percent of the total homeland. The lowland is a flat, grassy plain with only sparse scrub and somewhat heavier cover in the river valleys. The plain is cut by numerous rivers flowing southeastward from the mountains. Since these streams do not dry up entirely even during the worst of the dry season, the lowland valleys are perpetually watered and are green throughout the year despite the dryness of the intervening plains. These lowlands receive somewhat more rainfall than the plateau to the west receives, almost always more than the 30 inches estimated as desirable for indigenous cultivation. During the rains much of the lowland is flooded due to sudden, heavy downpours, endangering the health of men and livestock.

Previous to the political stability established with colonial rule, the lowlands were frequently raided by caravans in search of supplies and slaves and by Masai, Baraguyu, Kamba, Hehe, Ngulu, and others raiding for livestock, slaves, and food supplies. This flat area provided little natural cover and was therefore difficult to defend so that in that period this area was far less heavily settled. The European colonialists found these lowlands ideal for sisal, which thrives on dry soil but requires a good water supply nearby for commercial processing. Since the land was sparsely populated, it was easily alienated to Europeans for vast sisal plantations which were worked mainly by migrant laborers.

2. MOUNTAINS.   About one-third of Kaguruland lies more than 4500 feet above sea level. This may be divided into a large continuous highland mass of very precipitous mountains in south-central Kaguruland (called Itumba) and many isolated peaks scattered over northern Kaguruland. These scattered peaks are better considered as part of the plateau area, but the highlands in the south form a large and distinct geographic zone. Many peaks exceed 6000 feet, some 7000 feet in height; it is a spectacularly beautiful and remote area. It is the source of most of the streams flowing into the plateau and lowlands. Its highest peak receives over 100 inches of rainfall, and if we allow only half this in the lower highland, the rainfall remains superabundant. Besides small valleys with level, arable land, the mountains may be divided into four distinct zones. The highest peaks are enormous outcrops of naked rock. Below these summits is a luxuriant semitropical rain forest of great density which has been protected as a forest preserve ever since German times. Further down, the land becomes very steep, alpine-type pasture, thickly covered with grass and almost devoid of trees and scrub. These were probably deforested in the precolonial period when Kaguru fled here to escape the raids of Hehe, Masai, Baraguyu, and Arab caravaneers. (This description also applies in miniature to the higher, isolated peaks in northern Kaguru-

land.) Below this pastureland are foothills covered by dense scrub thickets, land too rocky and dry for anything but limited grazing. While temperature is not an important factor influencing settlement in the lowlands and plateau, it is of great significance in the mountains. There, the long, heavy rainy season is especially bitter because of wind and cold, for it is between 10 and 20° F cooler there than in the plateau and lowlands.[2] The damp, cold climate is said by Kaguru to be one of the main reasons why many abandoned this area once it was safe to do so.

3. PLATEAU.   Nearly half of Kaguruland lies between 2000 and 4500 feet. This is not only the largest Kaguru region geographically, but today over two-thirds of the Kaguru live here and, aside from the lowland alien sisal estates, this is the site of most of the administrative, marketing, mission, and communication services in Kaguruland. Most of the plateau is low, rolling hills covered with thin scrub and dotted with taller trees and occasionally marked by wide stands of parklike woods in higher areas not worth cultivating. Across this plateau are scattered prominent peaks and eruptions of rock, spaced 5–10 miles apart. These rise to between 4000 and 6000 feet in height and are prominent points of reference for all Kaguru in giving directions or explaining the locations of their particular homes.

The peaks of the plateau are sometimes heavily forested, especially near their summits, which contain water throughout the year. Besides these peaks, the plateau may be divided into three zones: river valleys, bush, and wooded upland. The plateau is traversed by many streams which form valleys leading down from the peaks to the plain below. These valleys are wide, flat, and relatively fertile since they are annually replenished by alluvial deposits during the rainy season floods. They form a nearly continuous patchwork of cultivation. Where streams join or run parallel, such valleys may stretch several miles in width. Above these is rolling land of light scrub vegetation which has been subjected to decades of slash-and-burn cultivation which have given an irregular quality to the cover.

There is no serious water shortage in most of the plateau, although there is a marked decrease in rainfall as one moves westward. Thirty inches of rainfall occurs in most though not all years. Except in parts of the west, water for human needs is always readily available, and there the government has sunk bore wells to alleviate the problem.

But the abundance of water in the Kaguru highlands does not mean that the mountains are any more suitable for cultivation than much of the lowlands. The very rocky, precipitous terrain provides little level, arable land. Hillsides are cultivated, but usually without terracing so that plots wash out within one or two years. The soil is rocky and shallow except in small valleys, where streams have deposited small pockets of soil. In these small, fertile valleys it is possible to get two annual crops from many of the gardens. The long rainy season and cool climate limit cultivation to "wet" crops such as maize, tobacco, potatoes, and some types of beans. Millet and sorghum cannot be grown here so that before the

---

[2] In the plateau temperatures may reach 95°F in the wet season, although the daytime average is in the eighties. Temperatures at that season rarely drop below 65–70°F at night. In the dry season day temperatures tend to be in the seventies, night temperatures in the fifties. Lowland temperatures tend to be about 5°F warmer than in the plateau.

introduction of maize, this area could probably not have supported as large a population as it does now, not to mention the larger population it undoubtedly had during the slaving period.[3]

In the past only in the higher mountains were Kaguru able to maintain herds of livestock. The prime value of much of this area is defensibility, an advantage no longer required by Kaguru. Certain valuable cash crops such as coffee, citrus fruits, and vegetables thrive here, but transportation is so difficult that these are not economically marketable.

Much of the eastern lowland does not especially favor African hoe agriculture. During the heaviest rains the rivers may wash away fields planted nearby, while in the dry season the soil is too dry to be of use. Then some river bottoms may be available for cultivation of quick-maturing crops put in after the rains subside. Open grasslands can be cleared by slash-and-burn methods but are not usually fertile for more than three or four years at best. Only a limited part of the lowlands at any time is suitable for traditional crops such as maize, groundnuts, tobacco, cassava, bananas, yams, and plantains. Some cotton is also grown. Thus, the plateau must be considered the most important and typical economic region of the chiefdom.

This bush area of the plateau provides pasture for livestock and some land for cultivation which must be abandoned only two or three years after being cleared. Crops grown here are more dependent upon rains than are those in the river valleys. Between these semiarable areas and the peaks are wooded foothills which are too rocky and dry for cultivation but which provide good pasturage for livestock; such wooded parkland comprises nearly half of the plateau.

A wide range of crops are grown in the plateau: maize, tobacco, groundnuts, potatoes, beans, castor, plantains, bananas, and millet. In the drier west, sorghum and millet prevail over maize.

Nearly all of the people of Tanzania gain their livelihood directly from the land and are therefore concerned with one crucial annual problem—the rains. Compared to their neighbors, the Kaguru are favored in the distribution of rainfall, but occasional hard times occur. Kaguruland is subject to two pronounced seasons: a warm, dry season and a cooler, rainy season. The rains commence in late November or early December, reach their peak in February and March, and slack off until the dry season, which commences in June. From mid-June to mid-November often no rain whatsoever falls. The rainy season is, of course, longer in the mountains. The problem, however, may not simply be gauged in terms of the number of inches of rainfall in the year. Rather, it is the distribution of that rain. A year of heavy rainfall, if it washes out crops or rots a standing harvest, can be more devastating than a drought. We should not be surprised, therefore, that

---

[3] When I refer to traditional Kaguru crops, I mean those cultivated before the arrival of the Germans. Many important Kaguru crops, such as maize, tobacco, and groundnuts, were introduced into East Africa some time after the European discovery of the New World, probably through Portuguese contact with the East African coast in the early sixteenth century. Arabs introduced many plants, including many fruits and spices. Kaguru themselves insist that they always possessed maize and tobacco, tobacco being a gift to them from the ghosts of the dead.

Kaguru have long been preoccupied with medicines and rituals to control rain. The undependability of a good harvest every year and the relatively favorable position of the Kaguru vis-à-vis their western neighbors, and their correspondingly poorer position vis-à-vis their eastern neighbors, explain much of Kaguru inter-tribal social and political relations.

Within this relatively small area is a very wide range of ecological zones from tropical highland jungle, alpine meadows to thick bush, deciduous woods, intensely cultivated river valleys, and dry savannah. Despite this, the general fabric of Kaguru society remains the same in these areas.

A general idea of the system of communications in Kaguruland must be had if we are to understand certain social patterns central to this study, such as the marketing of crops, the transmission of orders and information between the government and various localities in Kaguruland, and the differential rate of social change within the area. The main east-west road for all Tanzania passes through the center of Kaguruland. However, it passes some distance from the main centers of population in the plateau. A fair north-south road passes through the eastern lowlands. Secondary roads in the plateau are poor, and the two roads into the mountains are very poor. During the rains the mountain area is sealed off to all but foot traffic, and parts of the plateau area are occasionally cut off for days or weeks at a time when floods wash out roadbeds or bridges.

During the colonial period, the European population of Kaguruland was limited to a dozen European missionaries and farmers; today only a few missionaries remain. In the colonial period perhaps 500 Indian, Arab, and Somali traders lived in Kaguruland, nearly two-thirds in the lowlands and none in the mountains. Today this number is probably drastically reduced.

A few words should be said about the nature of the distribution and composition of the African population of Kaguruland. Some 11,000 migrant laborers dwell in the lowlands, but these have little to do with Kaguru since they are quartered apart in huge estates. The plateau contains over two-thirds of the population. The mountains today contain less than 10 percent of the population. The mountains have about eight persons per square mile; the plateau, between ten and thirty persons per square mile, depending upon the area. The lowland figures are too confused by the estate figures to make sense. It should also be noted that about 3000 Baraguyu reside in Kaguruland, about 2000 Ngulu, nearly 2000 Kamba, and 4000 or 5000 Gogo—perhaps even more Gogo than this, depending upon where one draws Kaguruland's western boundary.

# History

Ukaguru is a land which has had very long and difficult contact with outsiders.[4] The Kaguru live in an area between several very different cultural groups which were traditionally at odds with one another. Although a people who place

---

[4] I have discussed Kaguru history and the sources for that history in more detail elsewhere (Beidelman 1962, 1967a, 1970b, and the books cited in "Further Readings, General Cultural Area").

a low value upon warfare, they have been forced to deal for generations with some of what are reputed to be the most aggressive peoples in East Africa, especially the Masai and Hehe. In general, the Kaguru preserved themselves by defensive combat from their mountain areas and sometimes by making temporary alliances with some of their enemies in order, in turn, to raid others, sometimes even other Kaguru. A discussion of traditional Kaguru history is better postponed until I discuss Kaguru beliefs in Chapter 4.

Kaguruland lies astride what was once one of the major caravan routes which led from the Arab-dominated Indian Ocean ports to the great inland lakes of Central Africa. In the nineteenth century most of the Arab and African caravans traversing most of Tanzania brought goods eventually to the island port of Zanzibar and the subsidiary ports facing Zanzibar on the Tanzanian coast. Nearly all such caravans passed through the general vicinity of Kaguruland, which formed a relatively safe corridor between areas to the north and south which were arid, mountainous, and dominated by warlike peoples. It is estimated that shortly before Europeans colonized the area, nearly 100,000 persons in caravans passed annually through Kaguruland, mainly involved in trade in ivory and slaves (Beidelman 1962:12). By the late nineteenth century areas near the coast had been hunted out of ivory and reduced of their easily captured inhabitants, which had been enslaved. Then, areas such as Kaguruland served simply as sites for caravan stations where traders could rest, take supplies and water, and organize locals for various subsidiary services. In 1871, when Stanley passed through Kaguruland in his search for Dr. Livingston, he noted the depredations of both Arab and African raiders (Stanley 1872:247). Caravaneers sought slaves and looted for supplies; Arabs readily sold arms to Africans and sought to encourage intertribal warfare in the hope of purchasing the defeated from the victors. In addition, the intrusion of aliens from the coast and also down the Rift Valley appears to have brought human and livestock epidemics, including small pox, rinderpest, cholera, East Coast fever, and meningitis. All of these factors led to serious upheavals and movements of local peoples. Thus, those who had lost livestock often sought to replace these from their neighbors' herds. Aggressive or ambitious persons, previously held in check by their neighbors with whom they were militarily equal, would begin trading for arms before their neighbors did so and would then exploit their new advantage while they could.

Arab and African traders benefited from the upheavals they sowed, and yet, out of self-interest, they also sought to establish spheres of stability along which their own affairs of trade and travel might proceed. It is a risky business to encourage warfare by dispensing arms and yet remain safe oneself, especially if one is involved in conducting vast, slow-moving shipments of trade goods and slaves across wild areas. In this sense, the ivory and slave trade of the Arabs was founded upon a contradiction in aims which caused the Arabs repeated difficulties: They had to create conflict and arm local Africans in order to secure slaves and purchase goods, yet they required stability for the movement and servicing of their vulnerable caravans.

In the late 1870s, the Arabs recognized and supported a local Kaguru leader in Mamboya (see frontispiece map) named Senyagwa Chimola. They gave him arms, cloth, and beads, and he in turn provided them with local labor, building materials, a building site, and food; he also allowed African strangers associated with the caravan trade to establish settlements along the caravan route. The Arabs recognized Senyagwa as the sultan, encouraged him to take an Arab name, Saidi, and helped him extend his political influence. During this time a number of Kaguru tried to exploit these local difficulties either by seeking Arab arms and support or by using arms to raid and intimidate their neighbors or to loot caravans. In short, as trade intensified, there was a profound disruption in the balance between traditional Kaguru political units (a process to which I give further attention in Chapter 6). This disruption afforded some ambitious men with opportunities to dominate groups on a scale unknown in earlier times.

Many of the famous expeditions by early European travelers in East and Central Africa passed through Kaguruland, but the first Europeans to settle and undertake changes in the area were British missionaries. The first of these passed through Kaguruland in 1876 on their way to Uganda, where they were then establishing a thriving mission as well as aiding their countrymen in wresting the Nile headwaters from the French. However, they were so impressed with the apparent fertility and healthfulness of this area (they were later proved over-optimistic) that by 1880 they had established a station near the Arab palisade and Arab-supported chief's headquarters at Mamboya in central Kaguruland. The missionaries hoped to aid their fellows as they passed inland, convert local Kaguru, and obstruct the Arab slave trade whenever possible. From the beginning they were thus in opposition not only to the Arabs but to those Kaguru and others who had benefited from the Arab caravans. However, they were consequently welcomed by other Kaguru who sought to use the missionaries (with their connections with the powerful Europeans on the coast, who had in turn intimidated the Arabs) against the new and radical political changes which were upsetting Kaguru society.

Missionaries interfered with the Arab trade not only by reporting slaving to coastal authorities (who had signed a treaty with the British agreeing to restrict the trade) but by harboring runaway slaves and by underselling trade goods to the local population as well. All these difficulties were compounded when the German colonialists arrived. Carl Peters, a German adventurer, reached Tanzania toward the end of 1884. He traveled through Kaguruland and neighboring areas and persuaded some local men to make their marks on papers giving over their lands to Peters and his newly formed trading company. Initially, these Germans arrived as private citizens without their government's official support. Their aim was to make the greatest, quickest profits without outlay of men or capital. As a result, they soon came into direct competition with the Arabs yet could not count on local Africans to support them since they themselves had behaved more brutally and rapaciously than the Arabs.

These German adventurers created considerable unrest throughout eastern Tanzania, including Kaguruland. Their activities were sufficient to upset the precarious political and economic balances achieved by the Arabs, but insufficient to impose any new order in place of the old. The Germans relied mainly upon black Sudanese and black South African mercenaries. In Kaguruland they sought the support of the missionaries, who tried, in turn, to dissociate themselves from their fellow Europeans. But the Germans enforced little real order; some coastal Africans even led slaving expeditions into central Kaguruland, something unheard of during the final stages of Arab control. An increase in conflict appears to have been the rule throughout the regions taken over by these Germans. In 1889 the Arabs in the areas influenced by the Germans found matters intolerable and revolted. When it became clear that the German adventurers and their mercenaries could not put down the revolt, the German government proclaimed that its nationals were endangered and, in a manner familiar to all students of colonial and neo-colonial gunboat diplomacy, invaded the land to restore order. With that, Tanzania became the imperial German colony of German East Africa. The coastal Arabs were defeated and fled west, storming and burning the German palisade in western Kaguruland. The Kaguru heartland was probably spared simply because the Arabs had still maintained a small garrison there, led by an English mercenary.

The first main inland military garrison which the official German colonizers established was in western Kaguruland, mainly to secure the major caravan route to the interior. This German garrison afforded protection to those Kaguru who had been increasingly raided by their warlike neighbors to the south, who, with Arab guns, were now seeking to expand their boundaries and seize livestock and women.

During this time of German rule, Kaguruland was divided between two larger administrative districts. Initially, each of these was about the size of New England so that the Kaguru portion of each was of little significance. As staff, funds, and communications improved, these administrative units were reduced to about the size of a small American state, such as Vermont. Even then, the shortage of European administrative staff led the Germans to appoint Africans to supervise local affairs. In Kaguruland these were coastal Africans with no local ties and little knowledge of local customs or languages. Through the years, such Africans have sometimes expressed contempt for up-country folk such as Kaguru whom they have denigrated much as some Americans denigrate Southern mountain folk by classing them as "hillbillies." Two African administrators, termed *akidas*, served in Kaguruland, one in the plateau area and one in the lowlands. These were in charge of securing taxes and forced labor and reporting serious breaches of order. The Germans also recognized some of the local Kaguru leaders who had been first supported by the Arabs and then later by their swashbuckling predecessors, but these were never given the support given to *akidas*. Because the area they tried to supervise was so immense and their numbers so few (even after including their mercenaries), the Germans had little direct contact with Kaguru. Trade continued in the hands of Arabs and a few Indians. But Kaguru were forced to sell some foodstuffs in distant markets or to volunteer for labor in order to pay taxes, which were soon demanded in cash rather than kind. Germans tried to develop cotton and sisal estates in the lowlands and built a railway spanning the entire country. For all these needs the *akidas* impressed Kaguru for forced labor, though they were only able to enforce such demands upon the less remote areas where they could put pressure on local leaders. At one point the Kaguru chief at Mamboya was imprisoned for failing to provide labor for an *akida* to send to the Germans for road and plantation work. These political changes checked the earlier, gradual trend toward political unity in Kaguruland and discouraged political contact between the remote areas of Kaguruland and those accessible to the Germans. German rule eventually put an end to most intertribal raiding so that the turn of the century saw a widespread movement of Kaguru down from their mountain redoubt into the warmer, more arable plateau and lowlands. This was the most dramatic and immediate result of German rule and made the Kaguru far more accessible to colonial control.

During the German period the British missionaries maintained a cool distance in their relations with the Germans. They greatly increased the numbers of their converts as they increased their medical and educational services, for they insisted upon religious indoctrination as part of both treatment and teaching. Kaguru were encouraged to read and learn other skills in the hope of securing advantages from the colonialists. It soon became clear that literacy was one avenue, for example, toward posts such as *akidas* or other political functionaries.

World War I had disastrous effects upon the mission in Kaguruland. The British missionaries were imprisoned by the Germans, and some of their converts persecuted. All educational and medical services to Kaguru were ended. Many Kaguru were seized to serve as porters for the German army (it is said that more porters than combatants died in the East African campaign). When the British finally drove the Germans from the area in 1916, the Germans burned the mission installations.

The conquering British took over Kaguruland as part of their new quasi-colony, the League of Nations Trusteeship of Tanganyika. They were confronted by a ruined area with sabotaged installations and communications, burned administrative records, and a hungry population which had been too harassed to plant and harvest crops. Soon after, the area was hit by the great influenza epidemic that struck down a large part of the weakened population, which had few medical facilities. The subsequent events of British colonial rule leading up to African independence in December 1961, are better discussed in the later chapter on political affairs.

Contact with the Arabs, the Germans, and then the British had several immediate and important advantages: (1) The opportunities provided by these outsiders allowed some Kaguru to dominate larger political areas than they heretofore controlled. Throughout the period of colonial contact there was a tendency for centralization, unification, and homogenization of a population which had previously shown far weaker cultural and social ties. This is somewhat different from the usual picture of culture contact leading to ethnic disunity. (2) The decrease and eventual cessation of raiding, due to Arab and later German and British need for order, allowed a major population movement in Kaguruland in which the defensive mountain population repopulated the plateau and lowlands.

In addition, the introduction of new crops, a money economy, European education and technology, and modern administration all had important long-range effects on the area, but these were less quickly realized by the Kaguru than the dramatic changes just discussed.

## 2

# Livelihood

## History

THE ECONOMIC AFFAIRS of the Kaguru during the 1950s and early 1960s, that is, during colonial rule and that period just after independence before radical new economic policies were initiated, are discussed in this chapter. By way of introduction, a few comments on the precolonial economy may clarify what follows. Before raiding was sharply curtailed by German rule, it was a major factor limiting Kaguru economy and settlement. Then the majority of Kaguru were forced to reside in the more defensible sections of their homeland where sorghum, millet, and other slow-ripening crops did not grow, and many Kaguru had given up keeping livestock in order to avoid attack by Baraguyu, Masai, Hehe, and others who raided for such booty. Colonial rule brought greater concern with livestock (though Kaguru had always placed a high prestige value on them) and more efficient utilization of land. The precolonial population had thus been sharply restricted in size and living area in comparison to the situation under colonial rule and, later, with independent rule. The other major factor of change was the introduction of a cash economy. Kaguru were forced to pay annual taxes in cash and therefore had to secure money either by selling goods or by entering the labor market.

The colonial regimes of the Germans and British influenced the economy of most parts of East Africa, including Kaguruland, in two other ways: (1) The colonial authority assumed ultimate control of all land and disposed of certain tracts to various settlers, missionaries, and others. In Kaguruland proper a negligible amount of land was alienated, and today only that given to missionaries is still held and even that no longer in perpetuity. However, in the eastern lowlands very large tracts of land given over to sisal estates are still utilized in this way though most of the original European capitalists have now left. In general, Kaguruland was little affected by alienation of land to foreigners. The areas devoted to sisal were sparsely inhabited and would not support very heavy or sustained traditional cultivation, and the two farms established in the Kaguru highlands were in areas

15

also sparsely populated.[1] (2) Europeans set up official markets where livestock and produce were sold to traders, mainly Asians. In this way colonialists were able to control prices of goods as well as levy taxes on certain males.[2] Many Africans sold produce and their labor to secure cash for purchase of various kinds of imported, manufactured goods, but this was too undependable for the colonizers. To accelerate the sale of produce, to encourage cash cropping, and, most important of all, to secure cheap labor, Europeans soon demanded that taxes be paid in cash. Kaguru began planting cash crops, tried to cultivate more than they consumed, and sometimes sold staples even when this might mean that they would later risk hunger themselves.

## Kaguru Economy: Agriculture

Kaguru gain their livelihood essentially through cultivation, and I therefore first consider this side of their economy. Kaguru try to divide their efforts between several different types of cultivation, both in terms of the kinds of land they till and the types of crops they plant. They do not like to risk everything in one area or on one crop. A drought or flood may ruin a particular type of field, and pests, bad weather, or a poor market may spoil hopes for a particular crop.

Kaguru classify arable land into four general types:

1. GARDEN LAND (*malulu*). Near every house are a few small gardens which serve as larders for food required for sudden household needs. These gardens have some staples such as maize or beans, but they may also contain some more valuable plants such as bananas, peppers, papaya, or tobacco, which the owner may want to pick frequently or protect against theft. The size and quality of such gardens do not vary appreciably from household to household and are of little significance for Kaguru economy.

2. VALLEY GARDENS (*malolo*). Valley gardens are the most important types of fields. The lower valleys are well watered and occasionally flooded in the rains and thus enriched with sediment. Of all land in Ukaguru, this is the best watered, most fertile, most level, and freest of rock. Consequently, a crop of maize will grow there within three months after the first rainy season planting. This is important to Kaguru for their food stores are low after a six-month dry season. Even if a person's granaries are not low, his neighbors' may be, and he may then secure a good price from an early harvest. Valley land has the added value of supporting a second crop after maize has been harvested. More maize, tobacco, beans, tomatoes, or potatoes may be planted in part of these areas. Bananas and plantains are also sometimes grown, often as hedges or to prevent erosion if fields front along a river. Since such lands have been under nearly continuous

---

[1] One farmer did run into conflict by attempting to irrigate from a mountain stream used by Kaguru cultivators below, but he was eventually defeated.

[2] Cattle, as well as maize, millet, castor, sunflower seeds, sesame, beans, cotton, beeswax, and hides, could only be sold legally to traders through government-scheduled markets supervised by a government official.

*A typical Kaguru field. The photo was taken near harvest time, and therefore the field is no longer carefully weeded.*

cultivation for decades, they pose no serious problems in clearing. Usually, only the remains of the previous crop and some minor undergrowth need to be cut down and burned.

3. FIELDS (*migunda*). There is no clear division between prime valley land and the lands which extend upward and outward from it. As one gets further from the rivers and streams, lands become less fertile and are used less intensively. In general the word "fields" (*migunda*) applies to any plots used fairly regularly through the years. Thus, the less-favored fields are those which are not flooded and which sustain cultivation for only about three to five years. These must then be let fallow for about ten years. Such lands are favored, however, during floods and wet years, whereas lower areas, normally better situated, may then have their crops washed away or rot.

4. BUSH FIELDS (*miteme*). In the higher areas land may be cleared and planted, but these are good for no more than one or two years and then must lie fallow ten or more years. Such land is poorly watered, often very rocky, and covered with trees and scrub requiring formidable labor to clear. Unless there are generous rains, little or nothing may come of the labor lavished upon such thankless tracts. Many Kaguru consider the labor required here out of proportion to

the gains, and only those with insufficient land would trouble themselves with such work; for most Kaguru such lands are of no economic significance.

Of course, crops requiring very different degrees of fertility and moisture should be planted in these different types of fields, but it must be remembered that one can never be completely sure what amount of rainfall or flooding may occur in any year.

Agricultural conditions vary considerably from year to year, about every third to fifth year being a somewhat difficult one, with perhaps a serious food shortage occurring every five to ten years. Kaguru, therefore, are wary of investing all of their time and labor in any particular field or crop. Rather, the ideal pattern is to hold a number of scattered fields planted with several crops. Even so, one of the major factors accounting for the interdependence of scattered Kaguru local kin groups is their perennial needs for outside help because they live in an area with considerable local variation in agricultural conditions.[3]

The fields of any one household are scattered due to the complexities of land allocation and the quick exhaustion of some soils. Scarce valley fields are slowly reshuffled as Kaguru die or move elsewhere, but the constant demand for land by so many inhibits consolidation. Since upper lands quickly wear out, new fields must be cleared farther and farther from a cultivator's homestead. Dispersal of holdings has both advantages and disadvantages. Kaguru desire to scatter holdings because of varying agricultural conditions, but there is another reason as well. Consolidated holdings are more easily checked by others as to their size and harvest, and Kaguru fear the jealousy of their neighbors. Furthermore, boundary disputes would tend then to be of greater dimensions, for if they did occur, they would involve fewer protagonists but greater tracts of adjoining land. For all these reasons, some Kaguru do not seem to mind losing valuable time and effort journeying from one field to another at cultivating and harvest times.

Rights to land are secured through a local headman, and his control of such rights is an important aspect of his power over others. Having secured rights to a tract of land, an individual Kaguru retains such rights so long as he cultivates it. If the land is unused for three consecutive years, these rights may be lost and the land would then revert to the common holdings, which are again available for allocation by the local headman. There is no problem in securing a household garden, but these are very limited in size. There is also little difficulty in securing permission to clear bush. This is such a heavy task that only individuals with insufficient land do so, and even these, due to the difficulty of the task, clear relatively little additional land. I have never heard of a Kaguru being denied permission to clear such land. These fields are of small importance since they receive little water in most years, and the immense amount of work required to prepare them is barely worth the small yields. Furthermore, the labor of clearing undergrowth and hoeing rocky soil takes precious time perhaps better spent weeding and tending other fields.

It is through control of valley land and adjoining fields that Kaguru political leaders exercise local control. Such lands are rarely left fallow long and become

---

[3] Such distinctions lose some of their significance in the drier western parts of Kaguruland, where droughts are more frequent.

available for redisposal only when a cultivator dies or when he moves too far away to use the fields himself. A Kaguru headman usually has only a few such fields at his disposal at any one time since most headmanships have only a few hundred cultivating adults and hence few if any persons likely to relinquish land or die in any one year.

In return for bestowing rights to land a headman receives a small gift of a few shillings, some beer, or other considerations, none of which is considered very large even by Kaguru standards. However, a Kaguru's obligations to his headman do not end once he has secured a field. A headman would have considerable difficulty taking back a field so long as it was cultivated, but he is able to show his disfavor in other ways. In any case, few Kaguru hold so many good fields that they would not seek more.

There are frequent boundary disputes between cultivators, and these are settled by headmen. In the larger headmanships these leaders secure considerable profit through the small gifts and favors presented by persons seeking fields or settlements of disputes. A headman is said to have a moral duty to give some valley gardens to anyone whom he allows to settle in his area; however, there are no rules stipulating the amount. Inevitably, this is a function of one's own position in a neighborhood, one's usefulness to a headman, and the kinds of pressures which one's kin and friends can bring to bear upon a headman.

The Kaguru practiced hoe agriculture for many generations before colonial rule. Iron for hoes was found and smelted by Kaguru smiths, but the products of this craft have now been replaced by cheap imported metal goods. Kaguru tradition also mentions the use of the wooden digging stick, but these are rarely used today and are said to have been abandoned as soon as sufficient iron hoes were available. Clearing of fields and bush is done with a kind of machete. Large trees are usually cut down and the stumps burned out.

Fields vary in size from 10 square yards to 3 or 4 acres. Most valley fields are between one-half and two-thirds of an acre. The average size of a household's total holdings is about 3–4 acres, although larger holdings are reported from western Kaguruland, which is drier but less hilly.

The proportion of good land held depends considerably upon a Kaguru's relation with his headman and other prominent persons in the area, but in any case it is limited by the problems of Kaguru labor and technology. Few Kaguru are willing to give up precious time during the cultivating season in order to work for others. Kaguru who secure cash through government or mission jobs or through military service have tried to hire labor but with little success.[4] It is beyond the resources of local Kaguru to pay sufficiently to secure laborers at such times. The only notable exceptions are a few headmen who put pressure on local residents who are particularly vulnerable (tax defectors or recently arrived aliens with no local kin). Until low-wage labor is more attractive to Kaguru due to overpopulation and waste of land, ambitious cultivators with capital can only increase their agricultural incomes by taking more wives or through the labor of their unmarried children, especially their daughters. If a Kaguru has another occupation outside agriculture, such as a local craft or employment in the mission or government, he

---

[4] They are often forced to pay wages higher than the government since government employees labor either steadily or in the noncultivating season.

or she can afford little time for cultivation. But even teachers and clerks depend on their wives' labor to maintain themselves since it is uneconomical for them to purchase staples in Kaguruland.

The central problem regarding labor relates to the work demands imposed by the seasonal agricultural cycle. Fields may be cleared and burned at leisure during the close of the dry season, but actual cultivation, planting, and weeding depend upon the arrival of the first rains, and with these, work accelerates very rapidly. It is important to dig and plant as much and as soon as possible in order to utilize the maximum growing season. If foodstores are low, there is urgent need for an early harvest, in addition to what one later plants as cash crops. There is considerable risk in planting before the rains begin, however, for the rainy season does not commence at precisely the same time each year, and premature planting may mean that a crop will wither after sprouting. In many areas before the first rains the soil is solid and hard and thus exceedingly difficult to hoe. For these reasons there is a frantic drive to hoe and plant at the onset of the rains, followed by intensive rehoeing and weeding. Later, when first crops wither, crops with shorter growing seasons are planted (such as beans and groundnuts), and labor is more leisurely. During the opening of the agricultural year in November to December, with the planting of maize in east and central Kaguruland, and millet and sorghum in the west, most Kaguru work from dawn to dusk.

Kaguru have no strict division of agricultural labor. It is assumed that where men are available, they will do the heavier work of clearing the land, but some Kaguru widows and independent women do this themselves. Both sexes hoe and harvest. Older children may help if they are not in school or herding, and both children and adults take turns guarding crops before harvest against the depredations of birds, bushpigs, baboons, and monkeys. Sometimes when planting, a Kaguru man will walk along ahead scattering seeds while his wife or wives cover these over with their hoes and feet. Some Kaguru say that this has symbolic significance (see the next chapter).

I have tried to show how a shortage of high quality land and the technological limitations of hoe agriculture combine to set limits to the size and productivity of Kaguru agricultural enterprises. Productivity is made further uncertain by the great variation in rainfall and flooding, not to mention the depredations of various insects and animals. These factors must be appraised when Kaguru plan which crops will be planted in any given year, what proportion of their fields is to be given over to various crops, and in which types of fields a crop is to be planted. A cultivator balances these considerations with the need of obtaining the most of both staple and cash crops: food crops for himself, his family, and any of his kin who require help; cash crops to pay taxes, fines, school and license fees, and medical costs and to purchase clothing, tools, and other goods which he does not produce himself.

## Livestock, Crops, and Trade: The New Search for Cash

Maize is the most important crop in eastern and central Kaguruland; there, over half of all acreage is planted in it. In these areas maize is preferred to millet or sorghum since those crops do not thrive in excessive rainfall and since they require about six months to mature, whereas maize requires only about three or four months. This is important when late or severe rains prevent or ruin an early planting. With maize Kaguru have more leeway in their cultivation schedule than they have with millet or sorghum. Surplus maize is readily salable so that in bountiful years it becomes both a food and cash crop. Consequently, the price of maize fluctuates considerably from year to year.

Government officers eager to encourage more cash consciousness and greater productivity in Kaguruland berate Kaguru for not planting more cash crops such as castor, tobacco, cotton, and sunflowers rather than maize. The most important reasons for this reluctance by Kaguru are: (1) The Kaguru distrust a market which they cannot control and which fluctuates in ways they cannot predict. (2) In years of poor harvest Kaguru are forced to purchase maize

*Kaguru harvesting maize.*

from Asian merchants who charge high rates (Kaguru speak of Kaguru who sold too much of their foodstuffs too soon only to be forced to buy them back later from merchants at a far higher price).[5] Other crops supplement maize: Sorghum and millet are grown in small quantities, but only in the plateau area for there is too much rain and too short a ripening season in the mountains. As one moves westward, the proportion of millet and sorghum increases. In the drier parts of the plateau and lowlands Kaguru plant cassava which is left in the ground until a lean year when it is needed. In some areas the colonial government required cassava planting to prevent famine. Unfortunately, cassava lacks many nutriments, making it a poor standby. The main supplementary staples are potatoes, ground-nuts, plantains and bananas, and several types of beans and peas. When beer is prepared with millet or maize rather than sugar or honey, it is very nutritious. Plantains and bananas bear over several years and may be planted any time there is sufficient moisture for them to take root. The other crops are planted after the maize crop is well underway and therefore do not draw upon the valuable time needed for maize cultivation. However, the areas where these crops may be planted are restricted. Plantains grow only on well-watered hillsides or along streambeds, while the other crops require more thorough and deeper cultivation than maize and, therefore, are usually planted in smaller tracts.

Since a Kaguru would like to produce all of his own food and yet also be able to produce a cash crop as well, a concentration on maize as both a staple and cash crop would give him considerable flexibility and safety from year to year. But maize brings a poor price in plentiful years, and in lean years when the price is high, Kaguru lack a surplus and may go into debt or sell other goods to buy maize from merchants.

Kaguru cash cropping has advantages and disadvantages. Some crops, such as cotton, castor, and sunflowers, may be sold at government markets, but Kaguru themselves cannot use them. If a Kaguru commits himself to such crops, he is vulnerable to alien economic forces. At the other extreme are crops such as sugarcane and tobacco, which may be sold locally in any year and at any time since they are purchased by wealthy, local non-Kaguru. Such persons, mainly Baraguyu and Kamba, gain their steadier incomes from livestock rather than agriculture. In between these two crop choices are food staples such as maize, beans, peas, potatoes or yams, groundnuts, millet, sorghum, and sesame. These may be sold at markets, though not at particularly favorable prices, but may also be consumed by the cultivator.

Since there is a relatively small local demand for surplus maize, Kaguru sellers depend upon government markets for sales and share maize profits with the Asian traders, who transport such goods to sell in town or on the estates. The government supervises these markets, but in the colonial period it was the Asian buyer who controlled prices. Consequently, crops such as tobacco and sugarcane

---

[5] A rough idea of the range in such variations in harvests may be had by examining government market figures for maize sales over a nine-year period. These figures are for Kilosa District as a whole, of which Kaguruland comprises about 40 percent, but there is no reason to doubt that they reflect prevailing conditions in the entire district: 1947, 2601 tons; 1948 figures unobtainable; 1949, 169 tons; 1950, 3980; 1951, 3468; 1952, 1570; 1953, 20; 1954, 1470; 1955, 4372.

would be the most desirable since these fall outside such controls. Unfortunately, these crops, especially tobacco, require such intensive labor and skill in both cultivation and processing that they can be produced only in limited quantities, doubtless a reason for their steady good prices. In any case, crops sold directly to Africans may be sold free of government regulations or market fees. Markets are not open daily or even weekly, while goods may be sold among Africans outside the markets at any time.

Kaguru livestock holdings are small. In no area, not even the mountains, where there is ample pasturage, are herds sufficient to provide Kaguru with a substantial part of the food they need. The overall average Kaguru holdings of livestock in that part of Kaguruland in Kilosa District are about three Kaguru per goat, about ten Kaguru per sheep, and more than four Kaguru per cow. Holdings from several households in one settlement or neighborhood are usually herded together, but small stock are returned to their individual owners each night. Many households have a dozen or so goats and sheep, while a few elders have built up herds of over a hundred animals. Cooperation in such livestock herding is one of the few daily economic activities shared by Kaguru living in one neighborhood but different households. These herds of sheep and goats number from 30 to about 200 animals; cattle herds are far smaller. In the plateau few Kaguru own enough cattle to make a herd, and most loan animals to a kinsman or neighbor, who forms a herd of these pooled animals. Such a caretaker keeps these animals within his own enclosure and in return for tending them, he enjoys the benefits of their milk. It is impossible, therefore, to determine the ownership of all the cattle within any man's enclosure. This practice of livestock loaning provides some advantage to a prominent man and makes taxing of cattle holdings difficult for the government. Even when cattle are pooled in this way, herds usually contain only 30 to 50 animals, about a third the size of the herds of an ordinary Baraguyu, the semipastoral cattlekeepers who also live in the area. Kaguru livestock are not regularly marketed for cash, as are those of Baraguyu; rather, stock is kept over the years and sold only when some emergency arises.

Care of stock is usually entrusted to one or two local youths, who may receive payment from the owners. The more livestock a Kaguru controls, the more he must depend upon local political leaders, but also, the more able he is to provide occasional favors to secure such support. Kaguru herds trespass upon valley fields and sometimes cause considerable damage to crops as they go to and from water points. A livestock owner on good terms with local leaders need not fear any severe fines for such offenses, and he may even succeed in blaming such damages onto herdsmen from other tribal groups.

Nearly every Kaguru household has a small flock of chickens and a few households have ducks. Chickens are the major source of quick payment and the usual gift to or by visitors. They are never raised in numbers substantial enough to provide an income.

Few Kaguru can hope to gain any large or regular income directly from agriculture or herding. If a Kaguru desires wealth, for its own sake and to control others, he must seek it elsewhere. Even if a Kaguru has obtained some cash, such as from military mustering-out pay, work in town, or wages as a government or mission employee, he cannot invest it in the land. Aside from a hoe (which costs

*Kaguru (right) and Baraguyu (left) competing to drive livestock into an auction pit at a Native Authority market.*

less than a dollar), there is no equipment required for cultivation. Land cannot be purchased, and no more may be held than is actually used. Sometimes land is cleared or harvested by several neighbors or kin, but this must always be reciprocated and is more a matter of sociability in working together than efficiency since each man spends about the same total hours in field labor. An educated man might use his savings to secure additional wives to cultivate more land, but in most cases this is not possible because his prosperity rests upon his education and employment as a Christian. Even if he may be ready to do so, his present wife may refuse or he may find that only less educated women, not conforming to his own view of his status, are willing to enter a "pagan" marriage arrangement. However, there are other means for investment open to Kaguru which involve higher profits and involve less work and more prestige since Kaguru associate wealth, such as that of Europeans and Asians, with persons who do not cultivate at all.

A few Kaguru are distinguished as craftsmen, such as men who are fine woodcarvers of stools, combs, bows, and arrowshafts, or men skilled as herbalists, or women who weave fine baskets and mats or make fine pottery; in the past some men smelted and forged iron and a few still do repairwork on iron tools. No Kaguru can subsist entirely on crafts, however, and as a rule, such work is pursued only during the dry season after harvest. It is then too that repairs to houses are undertaken. However, none of these occupations is pursued full time even then, and the dry season is essentially a time of leisure and visiting. This is, however,

*Kaguru woman with her pot of beer at a beer club.*

truer for men than women, for women must prepare food, fetch water and fire-wood, and tend children year-round. House building is done by men, usually as a cooperative affair during the final stages, with the visiting men working in return for beer. Such communal work is entered into essentially for comradeship and pleasure since a lone man can do most of the work himself, and even the final stages could be completed by a man and one other person such as his son or wife.

The few Kaguru who might be called wealthy have attained their prosperity through one or more of the following three activities: brewing beer, petty trade, or some skill acquired through education. Each of these activities will now be considered in more detail.

Brewing beer provides large and quick profits and involves relatively little skill. By Kaguru custom women should brew, and it is considered degrading for men to do so, although there is no formal prohibition against it. In most cases, a Kaguru woman uses some store sugar, millet, or maize. With an investment of 25–50 cents a Kaguru can brew 4 gallons of beer, which may sell for from 75 cents to over $1. A few Kaguru illegally distill spirits or use herbs to strengthen weak beer which has not been brewed successfully. The economics of brewing are complicated by government regulations. The government rules that beer may be sold only on licensed premises. Licenses are expensive by Kaguru standards, about $2.50 per day (30 shillings). In 1957–1958 the government forbade all brewing during the cultivating season except on weekends. It was maintained that this regulation was necessary to prevent neglect of cultivation and depletion of grain reserves before harvests were in; officials did not recognize that beer sales were the main source of cash for many people at that season.

These regulations were enforced by local Kaguru officials who, in turn, were rarely checked by their superiors. In most neighborhoods two or three Kaguru brew beer on any day, even when brewing is forbidden. Then, they sell indoors, making small gifts of cash, beer, or their sexual favors to the local official or one of his supporters who might otherwise report them.

Many of those who purchase beer are not Kaguru, most being Baraguyu with a long tradition of conflict with Kaguru (Beidelman 1961b). Consequently, beer clubs are often scenes of brawls. For this reason, too, it is important to have the support of local officials whose help may be needed in settling or concealing such difficulties and in backing up club owners and beer sellers against unruly, alien buyers. Even during the season of legal sales, some sell secretly to avoid paying license fees, but headmen are then far less tolerant since they themselves often have covert relations with the entrepreneurs running legal beer clubs. During the legal beer-brewing season a few Kaguru purchase licenses and invite local women who have made beer to sell at their clubs. In return they collect a small payment from each woman. In these beer clubs up to ten or twenty women, including the wife of the licensee, may sell. Such clubs are usually well patronized; many Baraguyu and some Kaguru may travel as far as 5 miles a day in search of good beer, pretty brewers, and a circle of interesting drinking partners. The profit from such clubs is large by Kaguru standards, often involving total sales for one day larger than most individual Kaguru make in cash annually. Beer brewing is a profitable and relatively simple task which may be undertaken by any woman. Because of government regulations and the way these are enforced, a large share of the profits goes to headmen and entrepreneurs with political connections rather than to the brewers themselves.

Some Kaguru try to invest their savings in trade. All shops are of the same type, varying only in the scope of goods sold. There are no specialized shops such as we know. Capital, even for a small shop, involves $40–50. In addition to a trading license (about $3 per year), a shopkeeper may require tables, chairs, scales, scissors, rulers, and so forth. If further cash is available, the best investment would be a sewing machine, but this would in turn mean either that the owner knows elementary tailoring or that he employs someone who does. This converts a shop into a miniature factory, which produces trousers, shirts, shorts, and dresses. There are only two large shops run by Kaguru in Kilosa District, but about thirty small shops, often within homes, are scattered throughout Kaguruland (Kilosa District). At the end of my first fieldtrip (1958) several Kaguru and Ngulu combined to open the first African-owned flour mill in the chiefdom, which was patronized by many Kaguru women who disliked the chore of pounding grain by hand. Today several mills are said to flourish.

One of the greatest obstacles to Africans entering trade is that those activities which provide substantial resources in cash with which to engage in trade or beer-club owning involve statuses which impede business. Nearly all of the Kaguru and Ngulu with any capital are or were employed by the government or the mission. Those who have retired from such jobs have few outside sources of further capital. Even if they are lucky enough to be pensioned, their income is small. This means that a novice trader has little margin for error, and one miscalculation can end in ruin. Those still employed are even more restricted; although they continue to secure capital, they are forbidden to engage actively in commerce. The colonial government discouraged commerce by officials and employees as constituting a conflict in duties; the mission continues to discourage it as a worldly indulgence, though Kaguru are quick to suggest other reasons for such prohibitions. As a result, many ambitious men have been forced to use kin, wives, or others as "fronts" to operate businesses, even though these sometimes have proved inept or untrustworthy.

The main difficulty faced by aspirant shopkeepers is securing store goods from town, 60–150 miles away, at prices low enough to compete with Asian traders. Since no shopkeeper owns his own truck, arrangements must be made with Asian competitors or with African drivers of government transport. In the first case this can only work if he can find an Asian trucker who passes through his own area but who is destined for a more distant area where the African shopkeeper would not be in competition. In the second case it requires bribes since government drivers should not engage in commercial activities. Furthermore, unless the African owner can also buy produce, his profits will be low. Unlike his Asian competitors, he lacks capital and ties with retailers on the coast. Asians often operate over large areas through kin and religious ties, but they are allowed by the government to trade only at certain market centers with the result that African shops (sometimes serving as fronts for Asian traders) spring up in the more remote, less profitable areas. Thus, it is very difficult for African traders to compete with Asian traders with their larger capital, better training, and wider connections. One obvious way to meet the competition is to extend buying credit to local persons Asians would not accept as creditors, but this is a dangerous game which can lead to ruin.

Many are unable to open shops but nevertheless engage in trade. Some purchase a few pieces of cloth, combs, sugar, and other items and then bicycle to remote, underpopulated areas where no shop could succeed. Others sell tobacco, sugarcane, honey, or handicrafts (baskets, winnowing trays, knives, razors, arrowpoints, and stools) at local markets, especially at the large monthly cattle markets or at the produce markets during harvest. Such persons should spend a few shillings for a vendor's license, but many do not.

Education is the only capital investment by Africans which is strongly endorsed by both the government and the Christian mission, but the sums required are enormous by Kaguru standards. For example, a year's tuition in secondary school amounts to more cash than many Kaguru cultivators earn in a year. Money spent in this way is viewed by Kaguru as a capital investment for which dividends may be secured through the future income or values of the person educated. For example, an educated girl merits far higher bridewealth payments than one who is not. An educated youth is morally and legally obliged to assist his elderly benefactors in their old age. I do not mean that Kaguru educate their children only for mercenary motives, but education is prized by those with wealth because it is a guarantee of future economic security. The greater a young person's education, however, the more likely it is that he will be employed far from Kaguruland. There is, thus, an inverse relation between the degree a Kaguru is educated and the access which those who supported him will have to him after he succeeds.

It is difficult to determine the real income of Kaguru government headmen and chiefs since a considerable part of their income is in gifts and bribes. The official salaries of these men would not place them in the thousand-shilling category, except in the case of the paramount chief and subchiefs. Yet not even the paramount chief's salary surpasses that of many of the teachers, inspectors, rural medical aids, and others in the area; even local clerks and scouts usually receive higher salaries than the headmen in whose areas they serve, while the Native Authority truck drivers boast that their salaries plus bribes from hitchhikers and others total more than the income even of chiefs.

Educated Kaguru who work for the government or the Christian mission often are posted outside their home areas and sometimes even outside Kaguruland, and they may be transferred from post to post. It is therefore difficult for them to use their wealth to build up local support. With education these persons assume new standards of living which inhibit saving. Wealth makes these people somewhat free of their kin and neighbors and often enables them to be relatively independent of local political leaders as well since they need not rely on them for housing or land, which is usually furnished directly by the government or the mission.

Those members of the wealthy minority who maintain traditional ties and meet traditional obligations with kinsmen and neighbors are usually those with less education who have gained wealth and influence only after a long period of work through receipt of bridewealth and the support of kinsmen and friends in political office. Holders of administrative offices are dependent upon the support of their kinsmen and neighbors, both to keep local cooperation and to meet the demands of their superiors; they cannot afford, therefore, to neglect economic obligations to such persons. In general, manifold skills and social ties are required for positions of power. By contrast, Kaguru traders fall between these two examples of the educated skilled worker and the wealthy, traditionally oriented elders. Traders cannot help their kinsmen as much as these people demand because they themselves require capital to maintain and expand their business, but they are dependent upon their neighbors and kinsmen for patronage in trade and therefore cannot antagonize them.

In 1957–1958 there were less than 200 local Kaguru who received regular cash wages. These were mostly employed by the government or the Christian mission, although a few were employed in Asian shops. Less than half of these persons earned more than 100 shillings, ($15) per month. In addition, Kaguru men could earn some cash in the dry season (about $5 per month) working for the local government repairing roads.

Very few Kaguru have sought to secure cash by becoming laborers elsewhere in East Africa, as has been the case in many other areas more densely populated or less favored geographically. At the time of my fieldwork Kaguru made up only about 7 percent of the population of Kilosa town, the district capital for the eastern Kaguru.

*A Kaguru mission-school class; the teacher sits by the center post and is one of the few female teachers in the chiefdom.*

I have indicated some of the means by which Kaguru obtain wealth, but I have not clarified how such wealth is distributed. Today wealthy Kaguru cannot be stereotyped by age group, though this was doubtless so in the past. The overwhelming majority of Kaguru possess relatively the same wealth. Less than 1 percent can be considered wealthy by local standards; Kaguruland may be considered rather poor. Until recently, the economic conditions of Kaguruland supported the power and independence of Asians more than Africans, and tribal minorities more than Kaguru. Conditions favored cattle-owners more than cultivators, local officials more than ordinary men, and educated, wage-earning men more than traditionally minded Kaguru. These advantaged men amounted to a very small fraction of the population.

# 3

# Cosmology: Man, Ghosts, God, and Order

## Cosmology and Society

Asociety is a shared way of behavior. We cannot get far in understanding a society before decoding the ways its members communicate their wants and needs to one another, and in order to do that, we must first understand the ways in which these persons see and define themselves and the world in which they live. In this sense, language is the central and primary problem in social studies, although by language I mean far more than mere grammar, syntax, and vocabulary. What I mean is the sum total of ways in which the members of a society symbolize or categorize their experience so that they may give it order and form and thereby manipulate it and also deal with their fellows who share this experience with them. Language, then, includes not only words but gestures, facial expressions, clothing, and even household furnishings—in short, total symbolic behavior. Those with a common language share certain common values and perceptions and thus form a moral group, a kind of church.

In contemporary social anthropology the study of such systems of symbols and how they work is called cosmology. The etymology of this term suggests that this word is a good choice. Two English words derived from the Greek give us insight into the notions involved. The word *cosmos* means world or universe, the ultimate quantity about which we can hold some kind of idea. The word *cosmetics* derives from the same Greek root and refers to something which makes one attractive, presentable. These notions suggest the double aspect of the idea of order: (1) It is something which unifies, which allows for efficient manipulation or use of things by virtue of the fact that things are labeled through a *logos* (word) and sorted into convenient conceptual boxes and boxes within boxes. (2) Order is attractive; the naming and systematization of the items of experience hold a quality of pleasure for us. It may be, of course, that what we mean when we acknowledge that order is both rational and esthetic is simply that it is reassuring to have order, for with a system comes some way of dispelling confusion and achieving concerted action. It should later be clear that I think there is more than this to the problem of explaining why ideas should "feel good" as well as "think good." If, as some have done, we define society in "moral" terms, then this moral quality has both rational and esthetic aspects. An individual is constrained and inhibited by his relations with others, but these others remain a major source of an individual's gratification and pleasures. It is upon the tensions between constraint and expression that morality is based.

Earlier I noted that in order to study a society, we must consider it as a totality and not just, for example, in terms of its economic or political institutions or its kinship system. It is the consideration of social facts within this context of totality that is the special value of anthropology. In a sense, this problem of studying totality is posed in miniature for an idea system. One sphere of ideas tends to reinforce others, though there is often considerable inconsistency or conflict, especially in highly complex and heterogeneous societies such as our own. Idea systems, therefore, are complicated and difficult to analyze. Furthermore, the life of the mind is not entirely constrained within language. If one relied solely on theories of social, verbal indoctrination, one could not account for invention and originality. Some sociologists and anthropologists still maintain that the view of history and the natural world which is held by the members of a society are simply reflections of the social world. According to this interpretation, society fashions experience into its own image. This view may have theoretical value, but it confuses and distorts our picture of the way the members of a society themselves conceive of their world since they see the spheres of ideas and actions, and words and the persons and things for which they stand, as equally real and valid.

Anthropologists are keenly aware of the great range of possibilities in human society. But few anthropologists have noted that the members of many small societies such as the Kaguru are highly sophisticated in their awareness of other ways of social life. I do not mean to suggest that Kaguru view their culture in an alienated or existential manner similar to the views held by so many contemporary intellectuals. But Kaguru are very aware that their own way of life is not the only possible solution to the dilemmas presented by existence. Most Kaguru men can speak at least two languages and are aware of other cultures. I refer in part to the ways of life led by European administrators and missionaries or by Arab, Indian, and Somali traders who work in Kaguruland. More important, since they involve far more enduring and technologically similar social relations, Kaguru are also aware of the ways of life led by semipastoral Masai and Baraguyu, the Kamba and Gogo, and the matrilineal Ngulu, Luguru, and Sagara, whose societies resemble the Kaguru and whose lands adjoin theirs.

Why then do Kaguru view their own society with satisfaction and pleasure even though they have had a century or more to compare their society with many others? Is it simply that Kaguru society is better? This is a difficult question to answer since most of the members of the other societies mentioned also view their respective societies with considerable equanimity and self-righteousness. The explanation lies within the context of the larger perspective with which Kaguru view and define the world. The particular evaluations which society assigns human relations, such as matriliny, polygyny, witchcraft, prizing of livestock, and ancestral propitiation, make sense only in terms of a far broader set of ideas defining the world. For example, men and women are said to have certain physical and mental characteristics; therefore, in order to deal with men and women, certain marital rules are considered proper. Human beings are thought to be selfish, altruistic, gentle, or vicious, depending upon certain situations, and, hence, the following codes of conduct are considered necessary within a particular society. In this sense, particular rules spring from more basic notions about the nature of the world and people. So among the Kaguru the various choices made within their society are the only ones sensible to them once one has made some of their general assumptions about the inherent natures of men and women, and what kinds of relations exist between the world of the living and that of spirits.

## The Kaguru View of Space and History

Kaguru say that God (*mulungu*) created the world, but they seem rather unconcerned about how this took place. Instead, the furthest back in time and space toward which they show interest is in legends which explain the origin of the Kaguru as a people distinguishable from others. These legends, as our own history, enable Kaguru to explain many aspects of why Kaguru society is as it is; they account both for various social differences within Kaguru society and also for certain similarities and differences between the Kaguru and neighboring peoples.

Kaguru maintain that they migrated as a group to their present homeland.[1] Most say that they came from the northwest, wandering at first about the lands to the west and south of Kaguruland, and then finally settling in their present day home. Some Kaguru say that the members of this migration included the ancestors of those peoples adjoining the Kaguru, thereby explaining why these people have many clan names and customs similar to those of the Kaguru. As factual history, such an account is dubious for the Kaguru seem to be a congeries of peoples who arrived in the area at different times from different geographical areas. But this historical legend makes sense in other terms. Kaguru sometimes compare this birth of Kaguru society to the birth of a person; as humans are born from out of the land of the ancestral ghosts, so too the Kaguru nation emerged from the north and west, two directions associated with the dead and birth. Some even say that the people marched in a column with the women to the left and the men to the right, directions associated, as we shall see, with femininity and masculinity, and with subordinate and superordinate status. While there is a general legend common to all Kaguru, this varies in detail from clan to clan. Kaguru may cite this legend to prove their common origin and thus explain their common culture, but they also use it as a means to account for differences in Kaguru society, differences which provide the most basic feature of Kaguru social organization. That feature is clanship: Kaguru are divided into about one-hundred exogamous, matrilineal clans (*ikolo* or *kolo* or *ikungugo*). Clan size varies from a few hundred to several thousand members. As I discuss later, membership in such groups regulates a very wide range of Kaguru social life, including marriage, religious activity, and access to land and political office. Kaguru say that although they may have left their original homeland without such social distinctions (no one stresses this point, however), somewhere en route clans came into being. Most clans derive their

---

[1] With a few exceptional cases (see Beidelman 1967a).

names from a series of events said to have occurred during the migration to present-day Kaguruland. Some clans are also said to be related to one another, and this too is explained through such legends; these related clans should not intermarry.

## Clans and Ghosts

All of Kaguruland is owned by various clans. Some Kaguru clans have several stretches of land which they own; some have only one piece of land, and a few have no land at all. Kaguru say that the members of a clan "own" such land, though this does not mean quite what we mean by the term. A particular clan is thought to have a mystical connection with the land. This connection was established by the fact that the ancestress of that clan was the pioneer settler in that area, but nonetheless, this is a mystical rather than a simple legal tie caused by first settlement. Thus, the fertility of the land depends upon annual rites (*tambiko*) of purification which lead the ghosts (*misimu*) of that clan to guarantee fertility, but Kaguru admit that ultimately it is God who bestows such good.[2] It is said that in the past a few clans gave up their ownership of land to others, but when they did so, they had to perform a ritual which separated their ghosts from the land so that the new owners could perform rites with their ghosts. Kaguru see the members of the owner clan tied especially closely to their land, but they believe that all persons who live on the land affect its well-being. All of the cultivation and other work and all of the actions of people mystically wear down the earth. Furthermore, the misdeeds of all those living there, especially the owners, disturb the ghostly ancestors. Even if there were no misdeeds or cultivation, the ancestral ghosts would still desire annual rituals in order to be remembered, to hear their names spoken by the living. If such rituals are not performed, the earth would be less fertile, the annual rains less favorable, and illness and misfortune likely.

Every year, sometime before the beginning of cultivation, those elder men of the owner clan who reside in their own country rather than outside assemble and collect a black sheep, fowls, beer, and other goods. The most senior man of what is considered the senior matrilineage of the clan heads a delegation of elders which visits members of certain other clans with whom the owner clan elders enact such rites. These are the clan's joking partners (*watani*). The owning elders preside over arranging such rites, but much of the actual ritual is performed by the joking partners. During such ritual these joking partners symbolically take on the impurities of the land, for it is said that this would be too dangerous for the elder clan members to do themselves. The most prominent ancestral ghosts are named, one by one, and also the nameless dead; those ghosts who are not specifically remembered are also called upon to help the living. The spot where the founding ancestress and her closest descendants are said to be buried is cleared of undergrowth—Kaguru say that the graves are "swept"—and beer and flour are poured upon the stones thought to mark the graves. The blood of any animals sacrificed

---

[2] Kaguru beliefs and ritual related to ancestral ghosts are discussed in more detail elsewhere (Beidelman 1964b).

is also poured there. Often a miniature shelter is built over the site. The dead are thought to gain mystical nourishment from the offerings and to be made "cool" or "quiet" and therefore unlikely to bother the living.

Although today such annual rites are still performed, they are no longer held as publicly as before. In the past a representative of every household in the clan land was required to attend such rites in order to be cleansed and to contribute some goods to those who performed such renewal rites. All of the hearth fires in the countryside were put out; a new fire was kindled at the site of the ritual, and from that other fires were then lighted throughout the countryside. At harvest a small token sample of grain or other crops was placed at such sites as thanks for allowing the land to yield food to Kaguru. Today clan elders still conduct such rites with the help of their joking partners, but in some areas, especially those with many educated or Christian inhabitants, very few others attend.

Besides these rites, the owners of the land are also responsible for ensuring a proper rainfall in the land. In many areas such difficulties do arise every year, but we have seen that everywhere in Kaguruland rainfall is always potentially a problem. Some clans have their own rainmaker, while others do not. At any time in Kaguruland a few men have achieved prominence as rainmakers. It is said that those considered most powerful reside in the mountain areas where rainfall is heavy. Such men are consulted by elders from any clan land suffering from drought. They are also thought to possess other occult powers, such as clairvoyance and knowledge of various types of magic.

These annual rites are a useful means by which the members of an owner clan enforce their rule upon the other residents in their land. Although Kaguru always speak of this enforcement in mystical, ritual terms, however, these activities are invariably the expression of the power relations within a local area; when in the past these relations changed and a clan's power was lost, ritual was usurped by others, who quickly put forward a new legendary justification for their powers.

The relations expressed by an owner clan are only part of a far wider pattern, for all Kaguru see themselves as tied indissolubly to their ancestral ghosts, irrespective of whether or not these are affiliated to the ownership of land. The country of the ghosts (*kusimu*) is far away—some say far above; some say far below. Ghosts are propitiated on mountainsides and in the bush far from villages. To clear or "sweep" the overgrown graves is to bring temporary, visible order to a physically disordered piece of space representing something partially outside ordinary society. Certain sacrifices and their associated ghost huts are situated at crossroads for the same reasons, just as criminals and witches were executed at crossroads in Europe, because these intersections belong to neither (or both) of two areas and thus remain difficult to comprehend and categorize into any single zone of order. They are a kind of geographical expression of "dirt"—something out of place. Other kinds of Kaguru magical practices also attempt to harness the power inherent in crossroads. For example, persons with headaches may wash their heads and then throw the water onto crossroads, or persons desiring a rich groundnut crop may throw some groundnut shells at a crossroad before planting.

Some tales describe the living visiting ghostland by passing through mountainside caves or through the reflections on still ponds. When any ordinary person dies, his spirit goes to ghostland after his funeral has been performed (see Chapter

7), but the spirits of evil people such as witches and sorcerers do not; their ghosts wander destructively over the countryside, endangering the living. It is important then that ghosts ordinarily are confined to their own country and leave the living alone. The newborn come from ghostland, where, it is said, ghosts have villages, cultivate, hunt, quarrel, and dance much as the living; but life and death there are a reversal of that on earth. By this Kaguru mean that when a person dies on earth, there is mourning there, but in ghostland this constitutes a birth, and all the ghosts celebrate the arrival of a new person. Correspondingly, when a child is born to the living, it comes from ghostland, where its loss is mourned even while the living are celebrating a birth. The ghosts yield up their members to the living and vice versa, each doing so with a mixture of resignation and animosity. It is thought that an infant's hold on life is very precarious during its first weeks, and Kaguru perform many rites toward the ghosts (see Chapter 7) to hold onto their newborn, lest they be taken back by the jealous ghosts. The exchange of personnel between these two spheres is channeled along lines of kinship. Kaguru form a community whose members, some living, some ghosts, circulate between these two spheres. This explains certain Kaguru attitudes. For example, an irate and despairing Kaguru mother whose many children died in infancy blamed her deceased father, who, she said, was lonely for company and was jealous that she had children while he had few with him. Similarly, Kaguru who die young without being initiated are never formally and extensively mourned though, of course, grief is shown. It is said that such persons do not become ghosts which one can address by name, the idea being that in a sense they simply never fully ceased being ghosts. The two spheres are thus separate yet interdependent. The members of each sphere are recruited from the other, and each sphere can somehow affect the other; the misdeeds of the living grieve and disturb the ghosts, and while Kaguru say that ghosts are only remembered when they trouble the living, ghosts want to be remembered and gain some kind of nourishment from the sacrifices offered to them.

All Kaguru, therefore, and not just members of owner clans, are involved in some forms of propitiation of ghosts. But those misfortunes which involve only a small number of kin or households are carried out only by them (see Chapters 4 and 5). Any serious or persistent difficulty may be explained in terms of intrusions by the ghosts into the land of the living. The dead are not sought out except in order to quiet or cool them and send them back to ghostland. For Kaguru an orderly world is one with a minimum contact between the living and the dead. Kaguru say that to propitiate ghosts is, in a sense, to propitiate God. One sophisticated Kaguru Christian compared the ghosts to Mary and the Roman Catholic saints; it is sometimes easier to contact and explain problems to the ghosts, who then, in turn, beseech God for help. This, however, seems inconsistent with the idea that the ghosts themselves cause misfortune when they are angry or disturbed. God (*mulungu*) is sometimes called *Mateke* ("the soft or pliant one") or *Chohile* (he who commands) and seems to have been a beneficent and a malevolent aspect. Some Kaguru describe him as being something like a man but with only one foot, one arm, one eye, one ear, and so forth. In general, Kaguru seem little concerned with God, who is remote; they are far more concerned with the ghosts. However, sometimes profound disasters affecting the entire country, such as epidemics, general famines, and floods, may be thought due to God as well as to the ghosts. For the most part, misfortunes affect particular persons and groups, and particular areas, and, therefore, these are more properly seen as reflecting the influence of the particular ghosts associated with these groups and areas.

## Divination

But the anger of God or the ghosts is not the only cause of misfortune. It may also be due to the witchcraft and sorcery of one's neighbors and kin.[3] Furthermore, even if it is established that the ghosts are responsible, it may still be unclear whether or not it was the misconduct of one of the living which caused this. If such misconduct is found to be the cause, then it must be corrected and good relations restored before the dead can be expected to lay aside their anger. When a Kaguru suffers from ill health or infertility, or when his livestock or poultry do not thrive, or when his crops fail for no good reason, he may consult a diviner or doctor (*muganga*), who will be able to determine from which of these possible sources his present misfortune has come.

Diviners have a wide range of means by which they may use divination (*maselu*) to see into the causes of events, such as gazing into bowls of water, casting stones, seeds, or sandals, or poisoning chickens and watching how they flutter. Whatever these actions mean, they are only mechanical vehicles for expressing profounder mystical powers which it is believed that these men hold. A troubled Kaguru will try to consult a diviner some distance from his own residence, partly to test the diviner's powers (he should discern the problem without being told ahead of time) and partly to get a reading free from any local evil forces which might interfere with a clear revelation of the issues. Another possible explanation for consulting distant diviners is that any group which is alien to one's own is seen as perhaps possessing powers that one's own group lacks. The very fact that such strangers need not and do not conform to the rules of one's own group suggests a freedom and power that one lacks. Thus, Kaguru describe the Ngulu and Zigula to the east of them as more versed than they in mystical powers. The Ngulu and Zigula reserve their awe for the people even further to the east in Zanzibar and Pemba. Diviners are almost always elderly men, usually with a shrewd insight into the workings of Kaguru society and knowledge of the gossip and past disputes over a wide geographical area. In any case, despite Kaguru insistence that a proper diviner should proceed without prompting, the dialogue between patients and consultant is invariably framed in terms of the broad structure and basic dynamics of Kaguru social relations so that the causes and solution conform to the expectations of those seeking help. Diviners charge a few shillings or even some fowls or small livestock, depending upon the complexity and gravity of the case. They often provide medicines, and they receive fees for these. It was difficult to secure particulars about such practices from Kaguru, but payments were sometimes quite high. An old missionary account tells how a local leader whose area was plagued by lions employed a doctor-diviner who erected a female effigy with mystical powers to protect the area. For this, he was paid a cow, five

---

[3] See "Further Readings, The Kaguru," Beidelman 1963d.

goats, a hoe, and four yards of calico, a huge payment for 1900, when this was reported. (Church Missionary Society 1901:120).

## Witches, Sorcerers, and Magic

Kaguru see the physical world and the social (moral) world as complexly interlocked. Ghosts and living people inhabit two complementary worlds, different in space and power, yet sharing a common set of moral principles. Witches are different; they are the physical opposites of humans even though they may appear to be like ordinary humans and even though an outsider may find that, in actual cases, the selfishness and quest for power which single out a person as an accused witch are universal human qualities. The symbolic attributes with which Kaguru endow witches and sorcerers[4] are usefully considered here since they help us understand how Kaguru see moral values through physical symbols. Witches (*wahai*) are inherently evil people. Evil is in their natures; they cannot change themselves. Some are born as witches. Others have evil natures but are born without witchcraft powers; these may deliberately set out to gain witchcraft, it is thought, through incest and cannibalism. Both beliefs about the source of witchcraft are convenient since Kaguru like to say that witchcraft tendencies are often inherited, yet they find it embarrassing and at times even self-destructive to believe that all of a suspected witch's kin are also witches. This is obviously touchy when one suspects one's own kin of being witches. Even when a Kaguru accuses his own kin of being witches, he remains sure that he himself is not a witch.

Witches profess to be good, but they enjoy evil. They do harm to their fellow humans, especially to those to whom they should be helpful, such as their neighbors, affines, and kin. Witches can only operate against persons physically near themselves; persons can only betray and frustrate one another in society when they are in fairly close proximity. Witches devour their fellow humans and share their cannibal feasts with animals, while humans devour animals which they share with other humans. Witches walk and dance upside down and move at fantastic speed; they are covered with white ash, go about naked, commit incest, and work at night. All this is the reverse of what is normal for humans. In short, witches fail to observe the ordinary distinctions and limitations of humans; they confound humans with animals, kin with nonkin, up with down, day with night, and shame (clothing) with shamelessness (nakedness and incest). What Kaguru seem to be saying is that witches do not recognize the rules and constraint of society, and those accused of witchcraft are those who do not seem to fulfill their basic social obligations to other humans. They themselves cannot be human; they fall outside the measure of men; they are animals. Witches are something like an institutionaled version of Freud's id.

These horrible qualities should make witches the objects of the utmost revulsion by Kaguru; this is true, but many of the wealthiest, most influential and envied Kaguru are suspected of witchcraft. Furthermore, Kaguru themselves often

---

[4] I discuss witchcraft and sorcery elsewhere in detail (see Further Readings, under *The Kaguru*, Beidelman 1963d).

explain unaccounted wealth or luck as due to witchcraft. Kaguru say that a person may be a witch because he does not conform. A social anthropologist might say that the opportunity for nonconformity, betrayal, and self-seeking are greatest when one holds power and wealth since these advantages put one beyond many ordinary social constraints. Kaguru sometimes say that it is difficult to distinguish between some forms of witchcraft and some forms of sorcery, both sometimes being termed witchcraft (*uhai*). Technically, sorcery and magic are like guns; they can be used to rob or to defend oneself, but in themselves they are neither better nor worse than their users. Sorcery can be purchased and sold, and in this sense it is separable from the character of the user. But having said this, Kaguru go on to note that some sorcerers and witch finders might be witches as well, for how can one tell where such knowledge ends? These experts often assume peculiar mannerisms or wear odd ornaments or dress which they treat in a special, guarded manner. These persons seem to be trying to mark themselves off as somehow deviant and therefore having access to special powers. Witches, sorcerers, and witch finders are deviant in both their attributes and power. Physical signs are merely the outer symbols for moral and mystical deviance.

What holds for men holds for animals as well; pangolins (scaly anteaters which resemble both fish and mammals) and porcupines (mammals with needles for fur) possess mystical qualities to affect human fertility and hunting prowess. Similarly, unusual or deviant human behavior may bring power or may turn a negative influence back against itself. For example, a woman who required medicine to conceive may let her newborn child's and her own hair grow long in order to counteract the power of those medicines at work in the child and herself. In contrast, normally, long hair is the sign of mourning, of a mad person, or a witch. In these cases, persons do not fit into the usual social niche, but whereas witches, mourners, and madmen are in a sense humans out of place in a negative, dirty, polluted sense, the long-haired mother and child assume deviant attributes for positive reasons since they are simply using abnormalities to counteract another power inherent in the medicines used to combat infertility. This medical treatment, in turn, involves another dialectic of abnormal conditions, one counteracting the abnormal state of infertility. In the same manner, a newly initiated boy's parents may indulge in obscene language and acts at dances held during the boy's seclusion with his circumcision wounds; such actions are ordinarily forbidden, but here these are thought to help the wounds heal.

Inversion of the "natural" order is dangerous at all times, but this is because it unleashes powerful forces. These are ordinarily held in check by social rules, by categorization through words, customs, and etiquette. One fights fire with fire; one turns force against force so that in certain unusual and important situations such acts turn back evil in order to achieve good and use disorder to reestablish order. Even more dramatic than the preceding is the example of a parental curse. A parent who is badly treated by his or her child might curse that child. Then the child would have continuous misfortune and perhaps even die, and misfortune would plague his or her offspring, if, indeed, any survived. Now such animosity and desired misfortune between parent and child are entirely antithetical to the morality of kinship, but quite in keeping with witchcraft. This curse derives its power from symbolically defining the child as no longer human or kin. It is performed in a manner which in other circumstances would constitute witchcraft: The parent confronts his or her child naked and calls attention to his or her genitals and then berates the child. Ordinarily, this would be a kind of symbolic incest. Here, the parent is symbolically saying that no kinship now exists between himself and the child. The curse's force lies in the power of the symbols but also in the weight of moral justice on the side of a parent driven to such a desperate sanction. This justice in a parent's anger makes a curse legitimate and not antisocial behavior, that is, not witchcraft.

As a final example, I cite a rite by which Kaguru attempt to remedy a field that does not yield the expected crop even though it has been tended properly and is not subject to drought, flood, or pests. Ordinarily, a garden is carefully protected from polluting acts; menstruating women should not walk in gardens, and sexual relations, while sometimes adulterously committed in the bush, should never take place in gardens. It is synonymous with their antisocial nature that adulterous acts are done in the wild bush, like those of animals. For the same reason, evil persons are slain and thrown in the bush, ghosts are propitiated there, and powerful medicines can only be secured and prepared there. Superior powers, good and bad, outside orderly society, are found in wild nature. However, the sexual prohibitions protecting gardens are reversed to cure a "sick," unproductive field. The owner and his kin and neighbors assemble in the field, shout obscenities, throw feces and garbage on the field, and make obscene gestures. This is hoped to restore the field to normality.

## Unusual Persons and Events

If we consider the way Kaguru regard certain kinds of birth and certain events in the natural, physical world, we can gain further insight into how they regard this interdependence between the natural and social worlds, as well as the power produced by any imbalance in this interdependence (Beidelman 1963a). Kaguru believe that one of the fundamental qualities distinguishing humans from animals is that animals litter but proper humans produce only one child at a time. Another human quality is that infants are born toothless and delivered headfirst. Any child not born in this manner is considered abnormal (*chigego*) and not properly human. In the past such children were slain or sold to strangers who would take them far away. The mother of such a child was considered to be somehow disordered and required treatment to restore normality; if she and her husband bore another child before this was done, that child too should be slain. Abnormality is also indicated by any unusual development of a child, the most serious being to cut upper teeth before the lower. Some parents cut their child's lower gums to encourage teething, while others ornament a child with white beads and other "cooling" medicines to keep it on a normal path of development. If an abnormal child were allowed to live, it would possess special powers of which these physical symptoms are only a sign. He or she would be brighter, stronger, and more energetic than his or her kin, but would sap this extra strength from kin who, in turn, would languish. Kaguru say that it is in order to protect the kin group that such powerful, abnormal children should be destroyed. Sometimes Kaguru refer to such persons as being like witches since they too destroy others.

Confounding physical attributes, then, merely indicate profounder moral and mystical disturbances which unleash power so that natural forces are no longer held in check within proper rules and categories. Kaguru do not try to explain why natural disorder occurs, but they are keen to correct it or, at least, take precautions when disorder seems likely. Kaguru recognize a wide range of clues indicating such dangers, much as radio static indicates a coming rainstorm. These various signs fall along a continuum of intensity, the most unlikely and dramatic events indicating the greatest danger. For example, a man stubs his right foot as he sets out on a journey, and he may simply say he expects to have good luck or may soon get involved in some business concerning his paternal kin; he stubs his left toe and he expects some minor trouble on the trip or expects some problems with his matrilineal kin. Here, right is usually associated with importance and paternity and the left with the opposite. Or sometimes a man may disregard these signs and then find that the opposite from what he expected happens; then, as a consequence, in the future he reinterprets subsequent similar signs in an opposite, idiosyncratic manner fitting his experience. In short, though there are conventional interpretations of such signs, these are only minor ripples upon the surface of experience and are difficult to discern and interpret correctly. At the other end of the sign scale are dramatic and extraordinary events. For example, if a wild animal which ordinarily shuns men, such as a zebra or bushbuck, enters a village, this is a conclusive sign of coming disaster. One sophisticated Kaguru compared these two extremes in the range of natural signs in terms of their specificity and urgency: Some are like letters written by people who want to tell you something but want to tell you their aims politely; others resemble telegrams that you send in a few clear, unmistakable words because they deal with something important that must be known immediately. Here, disorder in the natural world is inextricably linked with disorder in the social and moral world. Each sphere yields clues to the condition of the other.

So far I have mentioned mystical powers held by God, ghosts, and deviant persons such as diviners, witches, and abnormally born people. Kaguru also believe in powers held by spirits; however, it is not clear whether such beliefs are traditional to the Kaguru or the result of contact with Arabicized coastal people and the Ngulu to the east since these peoples have similar cults based on malevolent spirits. Such spirits, often simply termed *shetani* (Swahili-Arabic for "satan" or "the devil"), are simply evil beings of unknown origins which wander about the wilderness. Others are spirits of the evil dead, such as witches, who did not become ancestral ghosts. An inauspicious child, a convicted and slain witch, or a leper (a person whose body surface is mysteriously dissolved, blotched, and disordered) are not given proper funerals or burials but are thrown into the bush to be eaten by wild animals. Such persons cannot become ancestral ghosts but are doomed to wander aimlessly and malevolently about the countryside, especially at night. Such demonic creatures seek living humans whom they may inhabit in order to fulfil their needs since they cannot be remembered or nourished through proper ritual and sacrifice; possession of the living is the only alternative open to them. The most commonly possessed persons are women, especially young girls and women approaching menopause. There seems to be much latent sexual frustration associated with such possession. The usual treatment is for the woman's relatives to hold a marathon drumming session at which the spirit is danced and drummed out of the woman. Continuous dancing and drumming may well have complex psychophysiological effects upon a disturbed person.

## Male and Female: Society and the Wilderness

So far, I have only discussed two interrelated aspects of Kaguru thought. One relates the general sphere of humans to that of mystical, supernatural beings in an orderly fashion; the other involves a twilight sphere betwixt-and-between containing devious, peculiar creatures which, because of their unusual and jumbled characteristics, do not fit into the ordinary spheres of men or ancestral ghosts. Equally basic to Kaguru notions of the world is another set of concepts related to Kaguru ideas about life and sexuality. In oversimplified form, this can be presented in terms of the antagonisms and interdependences between men and women. A large part of Kaguru ritual and ceremony deals with the manipulation of ideas and symbols concerning these relations.

The easiest way to approach Kaguru notions about the difference between the sexes is to consider the occasion of their conjunction, the event of conception. Kaguru say that the blood of a woman combines with a man's seed or sperm to produce a child. Kaguru have several logically inconsistent (by our standards) but symbolically persuasive (in terms of their values) interpretations of conception. The masculine elements form the right side, the stronger side of the fetus, while the feminine, weaker elements form the left. Yet Kaguru also say that the feminine parts of the body are the flesh and blood, lacking real form, while the masculine seed forms the bony structure around which these insubstantial parts coagulate. The symbolism here is subtle and complex.

These physiological qualities are associated with a wide and rich range of moral values. Kaguru say that the closest bond that exists between persons is that between a mother and her children. This involves far more than the usual bonds generated between children and the woman who raises them. Kaguru believe that the members of a matrilineage and ultimately of a matriclan are linked through common blood. This is transmitted exclusively through women. Children share common blood with their mother but not with their father. This blood links them to the land and to other traditions associated with their clan; if they were to commit some grave moral offense against these kinsmen, such as sleeping with a brother's wife or a sister, they would collectively endanger all their fellow clansmen through a disturbance of the common blood they share. Kaguru say that all members of a matrilineage are equally kin and contrast this with the links which people share through their fathers, links which also involve physical and mystical ties but which, except for one dietary prohibition, do not stretch through time from generation to generation as they do for one's blood kin. Blood links all equally within a matrilineage; the seed of a father links one person to kin, it is true, but one's father's closest kin are his own matrilineage, not one's own.

Kaguru sometimes compare kin linked through blood to the fruits on a

*Kaguru women pounding maize.*

pumpkin or gourd vine, and they compare the flow of blood through kin to a stream. The idea of fluidity and continuity is uppermost in these analogies between matriliny and nature. In many Kaguru rituals (see Chapter 7) Kaguru associate blood with fire, warmth, liquidity, and fertility. These symbols are used at different times to represent the qualities of women. The warmth of fire is associated with the hearth and nutrition, but also, like fire, women may be dangerous if not confined; women are compared to streams and rain, which water crops but which sometimes destructively flood the land; women are compared to river valleys which are prized for their fertility but which may become dank and overgrown if not constantly tended. In contrast, men, like the skeletons which they provide for their children, give form, order, and regularity to a social world that would otherwise, without male guardianship and authority, be fluid, formless, and wild even though fertile and emotionally rewarding. Kaguru do not always express themselves in these symbolic terms, and they do not force all their thinking about all men and women into such polar opposites on all occasions. In general, however, such stereotypes are held by all Kaguru and are used to justify rules about men's control of women and about elder's control of juniors, who are thought to resemble women in their lack of orderliness. For Kaguru initiation of boys and girls is, in part, a symbolic attempt to correct or contain these inherent deficiencies.

It is a common sociological truth that in all societies authority is held by men, not women. A society of Amazons exists only in the imagination. But Kaguru are matrilineal, and this means that they set special store upon the affection, nurturance, and mystical bonds thought to bind a woman to her children. In the next two chapters I discuss this more thoroughly. Here, it is enough to note that Kaguru view men as controllers of women, but Kaguru matriliny poses a peculiar problem for men in that their authority is manifested through two principles which are ultimately opposed. A man is the head of the matrilineage of his mother, sisters, and sisters' children, yet he is the fatherly head of a household composed of his wife and children, who are themselves not of his own lineage but that of some other man.

Men are sometimes described as shepherds herding their flocks or as rams or he-goats controlling a herd. Both images convey the notion of a strong and wise person controlling subordinates. This image could conceivably fit both a lineage head and a father, but Kaguru associate the comparison with a lineage head. Kaguru speak also of men as hunters, as those who go outside the village, outside society, and conquer the wild creatures of the bush. Kaguru quite consciously compare men besting wild animals to men dominating women, and the hunt often assumes broad sexual significance for Kaguru. A man's weapons, his spear and his bow and arrows, are primary symbols by which Kaguru express male dominance.

Kaguru show this contrast between orderly, rational men and disorderly, wild women through folk legends. They try to explain why, in considering the world of the wild, one finds animals and plants resembling the domesticated ones: grasses which resemble millet, maize, and sugarcane; wild plantains which resemble bananas; game birds which resemble domesticated fowls; antelope, which resemble livestock. Kaguru explain this by saying that long ago God gave man

*A Kaguru elder with his bow and arrows.*

and woman the same domesticated plants and animals; man tended his, as was his nature, while woman neglected hers until they went wild. The fertility and power of women are related to a notion of disorder; it is both woman's strength and weakness. I opened this discussion by referring to the conjunction of the sexes, ideally, in marriage. Kaguru sometimes describe a house as a kind of model expressing a combination of essential male and female qualities necessary for a marriage and for children and their nurturance. Kaguru compare a woman to the hearth, the fire and the stones on which food is prepared and around which the family warms itself. A man is compared to the central post that supports the roof and around which the walls are centered.

In discussing Kaguru ritual, I note that opposites are sometimes combined to unleash power. For Kaguru and, indeed, for many societies, the conjunction of the sexes in marriage and sexual congress is so viewed. A conjunction of opposites unleashes generative power, but it is so inherently dangerous that it must be surrounded by prohibitions. Kaguru are not a prudish people, but for them many aspects of sexual relations involve dirt and pollution. People should wash after sexual relations and should abstain from sexual relations during difficult and demanding situations such as mourning, preparing for hunting, and legal cases or when smelting iron or brewing beer. Symbolic manipulation of these qualities is a central theme of Kaguru initiation rites. Circumcision of boys is said to remove the moisture-producing, feminine part of men. After this, boys become men, that is, become morally and legally responsible holders of authority; in contrast, women never become clean, for so long as they remain full women, that is, until they reach menopause, they are unclean each month and, consequently, a source of danger and polluting disruption unless they follow rigorous prohibitions separating themselves from others.

Kaguru cosmology is based on the idea that the world is filled with forces and counterforces which may be harnessed for the good of man. Man is conceived of as one with society. However, the control of these forces depends upon a careful respect and observance of the divisions and distinctions between various things in nature and society. In a sense, social man is that man who discriminates and works toward keeping all things in their place. The epitome of this kind of person is the elder; in contrast, women possess strength (fertility) and dangerous qualities at the price of not being able to make moral distinctions all the time. Deviant people, such as doctors, sorcerers, and witches, deliberately gain their powers by consciously flaunting such rules for separating the various elements of existence. The powers of the world are kept in check through the observance of rules and distinctions, but these same powers may be tapped by a person by deliberately breaking down such order.

# 4

# Clans, Lineages, and Settlements

## The Nature of Social Organization: Kinship

D OMESTIC GROUPS, neighborhoods and politics, which fall under what social anthropologists usually term "social organization," will be discussed in this and the next two chapters. By social organization anthropologists mean the ways by which individuals and groups are joined into various social units in order to reach certain goals. In Kaguru society the most important social relations are expressed in terms of kinship so that another way of describing these three chapters would be to say that they all deal with aspects of kinship, that is, with the social interrelationships established through birth and marriage. "Kinship" is a term much used in anthropology, and though it has never been defined to the entire satisfaction of many social anthropologists, it is a term which we all seem somehow to understand dimly, though probably without proper justification. However, this is not the place to embark upon a cross-cultural definition of kinship but rather to try to establish what Kaguru mean by those terms which, in translation, approximate our similar notions of kin behavior and kin groups. Unfortunately, in doing this we encounter in miniature many of the same problems we face in reaching a more universal definition of kinship. These various difficulties are brought to the reader's attention mainly so that he does not assume more order and clarity than warranted when he is provided with a simplified model of Kaguru kin terms and relations. The most serious of these analytical difficulties is that the meaning of a term varies with each social context in which it appears or, to put it another way, the same term or unit relates to many social concepts and groups. This simply underlines the remarks made in the "Introduction" regarding the problem of studying "total social phenomena." Compartmentalization of certain ideas and behavior into "kinship" or "social organization" may be convenient, but we soon run into problems raised by any analytical dissection of social phenomena. Referring only to the last two chapters, kinship cannot be entirely separated from the ideas and values that make goals and motives understandable (cosmology) or from the physical and economic character of a society since this sets limits to the behavior of persons and provides the "things" sought and exchanged between persons and groups.

In all societies it is useful to make a distinction between a kinship system and a kinship terminology. By the latter I mean all the terms or labels which designate persons we would call "kin." This invariably includes the labels attached to members of one's immediate family, such as the terms for parents, grandparents, siblings, children, wives, and in-laws (affines), but these same labels often include a great many other persons as well, often placing groups of persons into social boxes very different from those we use in our own society. The social anthropologist faces his greatest analytical challenge in determining the dimensions of these alien social boxes and the logic of the ideas behind such a concept.

But a kinship terminology is not a kinship system, although much confusion has been created by social anthropologists who have wrongly assumed just that. A social system is a constellation of many social groups interrelating with one another through common values and language, and, similarly, a kinship system involves a common language of kinship terms. Each person has many kinship labels attached to him, usually as many labels as groups to which he belongs; for example, he is often likely to be a father, a husband, an uncle, a son-in-law, and a father-in-law all at the same time. Sometimes these labels are applied by different people, but not always. For example, in a society where I may marry my cousin (such as among the Kaguru), my uncle may also be my father-in-law and my wife, my cousin. It then might not always be clear which of these possible kinship labels I should use on a particular occasion; each label has special connotations.

In Kaguru society, where kinship is the language of most social discourse, the particular choice of several possible kinship labels indicates much about the attitudes and aims of the persons involved in a particular situation. Anthropologists recognize this problem by noting that we must distinguish between the terms by which we describe various kin and those terms by which we address them. However, the problem is more complicated than this distinction at first suggests since there may be a wide choice of terms by which one may address a kinsman if that person occupies more than one kinship category in relation to oneself. The fact that kinship labels do not correspond to only one set of persons and groups but are instead situationally determined is a reflection of the different priorities in loyalties and goals held by the various persons involved, each holding multiple memberships in different kin groups. A kinship system then is itself composed of many different subsystems, and these compete for the loyalty of the same person. Conversely, a person may pit the members of competing groups against one another as these vie for his loyalties. The everyday language of kinship, especially where choices in labels are involved, becomes a useful key for understanding the areas of conflict in loyalties and interests between competing social groups. These labels indicate deeper, more enduring forces determining authority and power.

## Kaguru Categories of Kin: Rules, Practices, and Social Change

In the next section I present the basic categories of kin as Kaguru themselves see and name them. I also provide the general rules and values which
Kaguru attach to various kin labels. Before doing so, I remind the reader that this
gives only part of the picture and a somewhat distorted one at that. We have the
labels and formal rules, but we shall not know exactly how these are put to use.
Yet we need this somewhat unreal, ideal picture of what Kaguru say they should
do before we can understand what they do in actuality.

This divergence between traditional rules and actual practice takes several
forms. One involves space and time, as these account for the variations between
different people occupying different situations in time and space. Another involves
the changing social definition of the same person as he alters through time. All
Kaguru are well aware of the same set of rules, but they have not been dealt the
same set of cards by life. Their choices of how they play their social game
depend upon their particular social hand of cards. Some are rich, some poor;
some have many relatives, some few. Some may have far more choice than others
in how they may play their game. One may become aware of this variation in
rules and their use in the following way. If one stands atop a ridge in Kaguruland,
one can look down to see a vista of small hamlets which in turn seem to form
larger clusters of neighborhoods. If one descends and asks the residents of these
houses to what kin groups they belong and whether this has determined where
they live, one will get a wide range of explanations as to why they live where
they do. Residence is the outcome of many different choices which people have
made between competing kin loyalties, rewards, and punishments. Yet these
different choices refer back to commonly held rules and values. The positions of
these persons in space, "on the ground," are the outcome of an interplay of factors which gives variation to the interpretations of abstract rules. However, ideal
rules only make sense anyway insofar as they allow people to live and gain
security and benefits in the complex, real world. We can speak of these as the
kind of variations that take place in space, that is, when abstract rules are
applied to the variations in number, wealth, sex, intelligence, and so forth which
characterize the sphere of people and things. However, rules also vary for a person through time: A boy is subject to certain rules which change when he is
initiated into manhood; and a newly married youth with little wealth is subject to
far different controls by his elders than later, when he has acquired many children
and some wealth of his own. For example, the distinction between a reasonable,
moral household head and an unreasonable, unjust one is a matter of degree and
perspective. The definition is subject to much struggle and argument. A youth
may assert norms of independence; an elder asserts rules of dependence and
authority. The winner sees the struggle as a just victory; the loser sees it as a
triumph of unjust force. All kinship systems exhibit tensions and conflicts as
rules and definitions are applied upon a choppy sea of variations in resources,
number, space, and time.

There is, however, another, broader divergence in Kaguru rules, and this
poses far more complex problems than the first set which, after all, is a kind of

divergence found in every society. This second type of divergence involves the fact that Kaguru themselves sometimes present two somewhat different sets of rules or behavior, one in terms of how their system should have worked in the past and the other in terms of how it should work now. This is not the usual distinction which old people sometimes make between the good old days and the present. The past actually does seem to have presented far different social conditions than today, and many Kaguru are keenly aware of this. The present social system of the Kaguru, of which the kinship system is a part, seems a kind of halfway house between what made sense in the past and what would make sense today. Kaguru retain a language and set of kin terms consistent with tracing primary relations through women (matriliny), yet they have many rules for inheritance and social control which suggest that primary relations pass through men (patriliny). Kaguru themselves describe their system as having undergone rapid change; in talking about themselves they often mix these two orders of rules, the "should" of the past with the "should" of the present.

In the chapters that follow I hope to show two processes at work. In part Kaguru attempt to rationalize a system of rules which are and always were inconsistent when lived out, even if one accepts what they consider the Kaguru's "purest" traditional version of their rules. In part, the Kaguru system has undergone considerable change due to outside economic and political factors. In this case such changes have accentuated the potential lines of conflict and tension already inherent in traditional Kaguru society, just as a stone would fragment along the crevices and cracks which were present all along, even before heat, cold, and water were applied in sufficient amounts to split it apart. A major theme of the following chapters is the demonstration of the assertion that the basic rules of Kaguru society are rationally inconsistent and that they generate certain conflicts. However, my aim is not to show Kaguru society, in consequence, as unstable; still less do I intend to suggest that Kaguru society is not sensible. All societies work only if they embody inconsistencies at certain levels, for these allow flexibility by providing several alternate courses of actions in complex and changing situations. We may need rational models and rules to impose some order on our affairs and the world about us, but there can be too much of a good thing, and too rigid a set of rules or too rigid and strict a model of nature leads to social and intellectual atrophy. Thus, I hope to show that these conflicts provide the means by which Kaguru society has been able to respond to different problems and to suggest that if I describe certain kinds of social behavior and thought as conflicting and not entirely logical, it is always within a wider framework which assumes that these so-called negative qualities are the essence of social life.

## Tribal Members and Other Groups

Kaguru recognize a wide range of relationships which might be termed kinship. Relationship by birth and marriage provide a model for other close relationships of a more voluntary basis so that it is difficult to restrict the term "kinship" to the former narrower meaning. The only term Kaguru have approximating our term "kin" is applied to nearly anyone to whom one stands in some special relation. Before discussing basic Kaguru kin groups, clans, and lineages, I briefly describe four less crucial social groupings:

1. Although tribal membership is not usually treated as kinship, it has many parallels. Kaguru should marry within their own tribal group. In general, they view non-Kaguru with both disdain and distrust. However, this is to some extent mitigated in the case of other matrilineal peoples who neighbor them and whose customs and social organization parallel those of the Kaguru.[1] Kaguru say that to be a proper Kaguru, both one's father and mother should be Kaguru and one should be born and raised in Kaguruland. However, a fair number of persons living in Kaguruland are married to non-Kaguru. The degree to which a child of such a "mixed marriage" is integrated into the Kaguru system depends on several factors. Since Kaguru are matrilineal, the child is usually better off if its mother, at least, is a Kaguru so that then it is a proper member of a Kaguru clan. When the non-Kaguru parent is from a neighboring matrilineal people, that parent may have a clan name identical or similar to that of a Kaguru clan. Although this provides no entry into the political or ritual affairs of a clan, most Kaguru simply treat such a person as a member of that analogous Kaguru clan and expect the person to observe the resultant marriage restrictions.

2. Kaguru have a word *ndugu* (kin) which may be a traditional Kaguru term but may simply be a Swahili borrowing.[2] The term may be applied to anyone a person wants to distinguish as deserving special social treatment. One's family, clan, and lineage mates are kin, but the term may be applied to neighbors, to persons who help one economically or politically, or to drinking cronies. Kaguru say that if one encounters a person whom one cannot fit into any other kin category but whom one wants to flatter or ask for help, one may call him or her *ndugu*.

3. In the past, few Kaguru ventured out of their local areas. Within their localities Kaguru were protected through the network of kin ties established through descent and marriage so a body of persons would stand up for one's rights in case of difficulties. Some Kaguru maintained kin ties over wider distances, but where none existed, Kaguru had an alternate means of establishing close social bonds, not only with Kaguru but with other ethnic groups as well. This was through the blood covenant (*umbuya*) and secured sponsors, hosts and protectors for men who had to travel for trade, to retrieve runaway women, or to seek ritual or magical advice.[3] Unlike kin, covenant partners may be chosen, but they resemble kin in that once such a bond is established, it cannot be broken. The bond is established through an exchange of blood accompanied by oaths; here, blood is a supernaturally endowed substance rather than the biosocial link between members of a matriclan. Blood covenant ties were important in the precolonial period when raiding was frequent and strangers could be robbed or

---

[1] I have discussed Kaguru attitudes toward other ethnic groups elsewhere (Beidelman 1964a).

[2] This word means "male sibling" in Swahili but can be used in a far wider sense, even in Swahili.

[3] I discuss this institution in detail elsewhere ("Further Readings, The Kaguru," Beidelman 1963b).

enslaved; with the cessation of raiding during colonial times the need for such bonds ended, and today the custom is dead.

4. Every Kaguru is a member of a patrilineal descent group (*mulongo*). There are about a dozen such groups, each associated with a particular animal or its part, for example, bushbuck, newly born and still blind animals, and the liver. The only obligation determined by membership in these groups is refraining from all contact with the associated animal or thing. Failure to do so may cause mild illness among one's fellow members but not necessarily in oneself. Even this prohibition is relaxed after one has produced several children.

## Kaguru Clans

The Kaguru have about a hundred matrilineal clans which provide the basic rationale for Kaguru social organization. Kaguru have several words for clan: *ikungugo, ikolo, lukolo,* and *kolo.* As noted in the preceding chapter, such a group is compared to a root, a herd, or a running stream, being considered the element of continuity in the Kaguru social system. Clans have a wide variety of types of names such as Goat, Crow, Cat, various species of trees, Spoiled Beer, Beads, Rain, Messengers, Milkers, Quarrelers, Ravines, and Breaking. While all of these names relate to the origin legends of the Kaguru people, there is no conventional, general naming principle, and no placement of these clans exists within some scheme of natural categories.

Much of the difficulty in understanding Kaguru clan relations is due to the way Kaguru themselves use the words associated with clanship. When questioned about the nature of a clan, Kaguru speak of the origin legend, marriage prohibitions, and associated ritual and political rights as though these were all of a piece. In actual practice some of these are better considered in terms of the lineages which make up a clan rather than in terms of a clan as a whole. In actual practice the term "clan" seems associated roughly with the dominance of a particular matrilineal group within a particular geographical area. Although this dominance is expressed in terms of unalienable moral and supernatural associations and rights to the land, it seems likely that until raiding and population movements were halted by colonial rule, some clans were occasionally dislodged from areas which they held, and some clans, as they increased in population and prosperity, quarreled among themselves and then divided to become separate clan groups. Several beliefs seem to support this interpretation. Some clans are linked with one another and are forbidden to intermarry. These links are usually explained by the origin legend which describes how clans derived from a common clan group. Sometimes clan names themselves reflect these common links, for example, Quarreler Rat and Quarreler Tusk clans, or the Cornborer Anteater, Cornborer Wildcat and Cornborer Cow clans. These groups may once have been one clan which flourished to such a size that it was forced to subdivide; Kaguru legends take a line of explanation consistent with this interpretation. However, these links are somewhat vague, for although linked clans should not intermarry, intermarriage may be allowed after rites are performed to separate these groups symbolically. Some clan legends describe how certain clans lost their lands to others, and disputes and animosities between clans seem to originate in such affairs.

For the most part, when Kaguru speak of clans, they are not referring to the entire membership of the group of persons sharing a common clan name and common putative ancestress. When they do speak in this broadest sense, it is nearly always only with reference to prohibitions about marriage or with reference to the common quasi-mythic legends of clan origin. Otherwise, the term "clan" usually denotes a considerably smaller operational unit than this. One definition, perhaps the most important after that involving marriage restrictions, involves the political rights held by clans; this is discussed in Chapter 6. One point, however, should be clarified now. Lands are associated with various clans, and those clans whose lands border each other are thought to stand in a special ritual relationship. Thus, each clan is linked ritually to three or more others. Kaguru call this relation *utani*, (see Beidelman 1966), which is sometimes, perhaps misleadingly, translated by anthropologists as "joking relation," although this consists of far more than mere joking behavior. Most of these ties involve ritual related to incest, witchcraft, and death. *Utani* ties between clans are relatively fixed and involve all members of linked clans, not just those residing in the areas where these clans have political rights.

Usually, when Kaguru speak of clan affairs, they mean the affairs of a particular matrilineage within a clan. Kaguru call such a lineage a *nyumba* (house). This word can refer to a person's house or to his or her household even if the members of that group inhabit several dwellings. The meaning which interests us here, however, is that of the largest group of persons who can clearly trace their kin relationships through women, that is, matrilineally, to a common ancestress. Sometimes Kaguru refer to such groups as having a common womb or belly. For convenience, I call the largest such group a lineage and the smaller units which make it up, but which are formed by the same matrilineal principle, lineage segments.

Because clans are exogamous, every Kaguru is linked to a number of different clans by the various male ancestors who have married into his group (his father and his grandfathers) and the clans of the men who in turn are linked to these men. Basically, each Kaguru reckons his primary loyalties along two lines in terms of clan and lineage affiliation: his own clan and matrilineage, that of his mother, and the clan and matrilineage of his father, that is, of his father's mother. Kaguru say that one is a member of one's own clan, but only a child (*mwana*), that is, a subordinate, to one's father's clan and matrilineage. This paternal group is called one's *welekwa* [from *kulekwa* (to be produced, to be born)]. In everyday conversation one may address a person by his or her proper name, but it is considered more polite to use his or her *welekwa* name, derived from the name of that person's *welekwa*. It is quite impolite to call a person by the name of his or her own clan. Such etiquette probably relates to some of the tensions which Kaguru feel between loyalties to maternal and paternal groups, a matter on which I will say more later.

## Matrilineages

A Kaguru matrilineage varies in size. A few, such as those associated with colonial political office, may trace relations back through six or seven generations of dead, but even these clearly do not involve all of the living descendants of such persons. These are far from typical and seem the response of enterprising Kaguru who were asked by anthropologically inspired colonial administrators to prove their rights to political office by genealogies. Most Kaguru have shallow lineages, tracing their relations back no more than three generations of dead. At best, then, most Kaguru lineages only involve about twenty to fifty living adults, though some are larger. Kaguru speak of the lineages within a clan as being ranked by seniority; there is a senior house (*nyumba ng'hulu*), a middle house (*nyumba yagati*), and a junior house (*nyumba yasiwanda*). However, this categorization must not be seen as true literally; rather, Kaguru tend to phrase all domination and subordination in terms of age. There is often considerable disagreement about which lineages are actually senior. In practice such ranking does not involve all the lineages of a clan in some kind of absolute hierarchy; it simply involves the members of those groups which reside sufficiently near one another to be required to sort out and rank their interactions. In the past seniority was expressed through a group's monopoly over the propitiation of ancestral ghosts. In areas where clans are thought to own land, senior lineages have persisted and still undertake purification and fertility ceremonies.

In the precolonial period matriliny provided the recognized way by which a sufficient number of Kaguru might be organized to protect settlements from raids, to enforce the return of abducted or runaway women, and to enforce payment of bridewealth, brideservice, and bloodwealth, to defend fields and livestock, and to provide a store of common resources in the event of famine. The political function of such groups, the aggregation of warriors, is often mentioned by Kaguru as the most important purpose of such traditional groups. Kaguru claim that in the past jural rights in persons were vested primarily in matrilineal rather than paternal kin, yet the reverse is true in practice today, in spite of the fact that Kaguru still continue to speak in terms of the past and the importance of matrilineal affiliation. This reversal in emphasis of matrilineal and paternal rights and the concomitant disintegration of the unity and importance of matrilineages undoubtedly stems from the loss of any need for parochial political groups such as the traditional, large Kaguru settlement built up around a core of matrilineal kin. Today intertribal raiding has nearly ceased, and Kaguru may reside safely in individual homesteads apart from their kin if they desire. In contrast, in the past even the most quarrelsome kin are said to have tried to remain together when possible due to the potential danger of raids. Paternal primacy is here associated with fairly autonomous individual homesteads and households.

A traditional Kaguru settlement consisted of a core of men and women of a matrilineage with men and women of other groups attached to it. A useful way to understand how this worked is to picture this from the point of view of the elder who headed such a settlement and matrilineage. A wealthy and successful man would seek to make the best of both principles of Kaguru social organization; he would want to hold onto his sisters and their children and force those who married them to come live with him. He would thus preserve the continuity and solidarity of his matrilineage. He would also try to hold onto his own children and force their spouses, too, to reside with him, thereby preserving the solidarity of his own household. Though every Kaguru would like to keep his structural porridge and eat it too, this was possible only for those few with much livestock, many kin, and considerable skill in dealing with relatives. Many less fortunate men had to leave their home villages and take up residence with their wives. Many a man had to allow his sisters to leave in exchange for the bridewealth he himself needed to advance himself and secure a wife. Ideally, then, the successful man waxed on two fronts: He gained new warriors and laborers (the Kaguru word for son-in-law is *mukwe mulima* [affine who hoes]) in the men who married his sisters, nieces, and daughters; and he kept his own junior kinsmen, his sons, nephews, and younger brothers, as well as his female kin. In short, a successful elder would try to retain as many male and female kin as possible and draw in as many affines from other groups as he could. Of course, no Kaguru could have hoped to ensnare all his kin, but some managed far better at this game than others. Conversely, younger, poorer Kaguru were forced to marry out into other settlements and to seek their fortune only by a long struggle building up ties of obligation, loyalty, and wealth. The solidarity and continuity of one settlement was gained only at the price of the dissolution and discontinuity of some others. In the precolonial period ambitious Kaguru had another means open for solving their dilemma of maintaining domestic groups without jeopardizing lineage solidarity. Successful Kaguru purchased slaves, especially women, whom they married. Female slaves had no matrilineage to lure them back to their settlements of birth.

However, Kaguru no longer depend so much upon the members of their matrilineage or other kin groups for enforcement of their rights in property or control of subordinates. Today, such rights are interpreted and enforced by local courts, and if ties are still important between kin, it is no longer a matter of how many warriors can be mustered to support a case; it depends rather, upon other factors such as a person's economic resources and education and his relations outside the local community. Today the members of most Kaguru lineages are scattered over a fairly wide area, sometimes over several local political units. The lineage is no longer the basic building block in the Kaguru political system. If it still sometimes appears to be politically important, it is because of the association of matriliny with the selection of certain political leaders during the colonial period.

Much of the confusion which the alien anthropologist or colonial administrator might experience in observing Kaguru affairs derives from the fact that Kaguru, highly valuing their past, still speak as though they had cohesive matrilineages. Today the power and authority of persons within a matrilineage are determined by wealth and political influence and only slightly by seniority within a lineage. While a senior lineage segment remains in charge of certain ritual, this is of minor importance when compared to the more pressing economic problems faced by a lineage's members. These economic problems are solved by cash, and while amassing wealth is somewhat related to time and, hence, age, the cash economy operates according to principles independent of or even opposed to those determining traditional rank within a lineage.

An unmarried woman's rights (her labor, sexuality, and offspring) are controlled jointly by her matrilineal and paternal kin. These rights are transferred to a nonkinsman through the payment of bridewealth to the members of these two kin groups. Upon divorce, rights to a woman and her subsequent children revert to her kinsmen. Wealth received for women in marriage is inherited by both sets of her kin. Kaguru courts enforce these jural obligations toward women and minors, though they have encouraged the replacement of primary matrilineal obligations by those toward the father. Other traditional obligations between kin are no longer enforced politically (today this means through courts) unless they are phrased as financial loans and debts. There are moral obligations upon matrilineal kin to help one another, but these provide a youth with no way to compel his maternal uncle through a court to help him pay his school fees. Except for rights over women, bridewealth, and control of children, Kaguru courts are supposed to apply the same set of rules to criminal cases between kin and those between nonkin though a court actually tends to consider criminal assault, theft, or insult between kin to be more serious and, consequently, sometimes applies harsher penalties than in the case of wrongs involving nonkin.

Today probably the most important function of a Kaguru matrilineage and other kin groups is to serve as a means by which economic resources may be pooled and redistributed. Kaguru are individually poor, and even the most prosperous at some time or other requires the aid of his fellows in meeting the many demands which the hardships of their world inflict. Few individual Kaguru have sufficient wealth for readily paying bridewealth for themselves or for their sons' and sisters' sons' wives, court fines and costs of litigation, fees for higher education, government taxes in lean years, or unusual medical costs, or for surviving some calamity such as a livestock epidemic or the destruction of houses or granaries. It is the affairs of bridewealth, above all else, which today lead Kaguru to emphasize the need for the support of kin; this is discussed in the next chapter.

# Settlements

Much of Kaguruland is composed of a network of villages ever more widely spaced the further they are distributed from the fertile river valleys. Between them is a crisscross of paths to gardens and other village and many livestock tracks where herders route stock to water points. Often one can see six or seven hamlets or separate homesteads as one looks out from a settlement. Kaguru have no proper word for neighborhood (some use "Kaguruized" Swahili, *chijiji* [hamlet]), but I apply the term "neighborhood" to the cluster of settlements one can see from one's own home or can readily reach in a 10-minute walk. Kaguruland is a patchwork of overlapping circles of contact between settlements, each settlement having its unique configuration of contacts with other settlements. These ties are informal, and no special rules exist for the interaction between settlements as wholes. Yet people of such neighborhoods are bound together by common issues and problems; most but not all are under the same political headman; most have fields and gardens which bound one another; some pool their livestock for convenient herding by local herdboys; most drink at the same local beer clubs, attend local dances, funerals, and marriage celebrations, and are concerned with the common tasks of maintaining local paths clear of brush, fetching water, keeping water points clean, and guarding against predatory animals.

The picture just presented here is accurate for the plateau area, where most Kaguru live, but there are many areas which are somewhat different. For example, in the high mountain areas hamlets are more widely scattered and difficult of access. These are built atop ridges, while fields and water lie far below in the valleys. Travel from one hamlet to another involves exhausting hiking up and down steep hill paths. In the drier areas of western Kaguruland hamlets are widely dispersed and do not follow the contours of any dominating natural features since no such features prevail. In the past settlements of twenty to forty houses were reported, but today the average hamlet contains only three or four houses, and lone homesteads are fairly common. Some larger settlements still occur, but usually these are the outcome of modern conditions rather than survivors of past tradition. Today large settlements of thirty, forty, or even fifty houses are found along roads where shops and markets have been built, near government administrative centers along with courts, dispensaries, and schools, or near missions.

To a stranger the number of houses in a Kaguru hamlet may give a false impression regarding the number of persons inhabiting a settlement. Kaguru custom proscribes many kin from sleeping under one roof. Thus, no initiated person may reside in the same house with more than one other initiated person of the opposite sex. This means that a man with several wives must build a separate dwelling for each. A married couple cannot simply take in a widowed or divorced relative, but must see to it that such a person has his or her own house. Once a couple has children who reach adolescence and are initiated, these children cannot sleep in the same house with their parents, but must sleep in a boy's house (*isepo*) or girl's house (*ibweti*). One family may therefore require three or four houses, depending upon what stage its members have reached in the life cycle.

Besides these human dwellings, some Kaguru construct a separate dry season granary or platform (*itanda*) on which harvests may dry before storage indoors. Some also build a small house (*suli*) for goats and sheep and a corral (*idewa*) for livestock, especially if they are lucky enough to have a large herd of small stock or some cattle.

A Kaguru house reflects its inhabitants' attitudes about social change and their community. The accustomed eye can tell about a house owner and his or her life style and attitudes just as one can do by observing a house in a conventional American suburb. For example, some hamlets are neat and have obviously been swept each day, while others abound in refuse. Some hamlets are left in disorder except during special occasions, while others are regularly tended. Not only are such accumulations esthetically unsightly but they are uncomfortable as well, since Kaguru, especially women and children, spend many hours each day working, playing, and gossiping in the cleared, open area (*lugha*) between houses. Each Kaguru house has a generous overhang of roof, and here families do their daily household chores, visit, and eat. Similarly, some Kaguru houses are swept daily inside, while others are less tidy. Since Kaguru homes are small and crowded with persons, utensils, foodstores, poultry, and sometimes livestock, tidiness is important. During the rainy season undergrowth must also be cleared from around the edges of a settlement to prevent encroachment of bush and vermin.

All Kaguru hamlets have certain areas for refuse which are also sometimes used as latrines. It is said that one can sometimes judge a hamlet by how

*A Kaguru settlement.*

discretely and distantly these are situated from the living area. Today some Kaguru have built special latrines fenced off from view. These dirty areas are actual and symbolic wastelands, being neither fully incorporated into communal space nor part of nature and the bush.

A Kaguru house (*nyumba*) may be of many styles, reflecting the sophistication and income of the owner. The most sophisticated are constructed of mud or cement brick and have wooden doors with padlocks, sheet-metal roofs, and cement floors. Government and mission houses are often constructed of cement block, and some houses of all types are whitewashed with lime. All Kaguru houses have carefully shuttered windows or no windows at all; this is said to be due to fear of witches, although in general Kaguru strive to conceal affairs inside their homes. Every house has a large, shelflike store or granary (*kano*) within; rain and thieves prevent footstuffs from being stored outside. As a result, many pests are attracted, and rats and mice are a serious problem, figuring prominently in Kaguru folklore and anecdotes. Poultry, sheep, and goats, if they are few, are usually kept within a house.

The form of a Kaguru house varies greatly, being the reflection in part of the owner's modern or conservative attitudes and in part of geographical location. In the past, when raiding prevailed, a low, easily defensible house complex (*tembe*) was built. At its simplest, this is a narrow, long, rectangular house made of wooden beams reinforced with dried earth and with a flat, earthen roof. Roofs are low so that one cannot stand upright within. The simplest hamlet would consist of one such rectangle. Then, as additional dwelling units are required, these would be joined to the first to form, first an L, then a U, and finally a large rectangular enclosure with its various entries opening onto a common court. Until it is expanded to form its own cattle corral, a supplementary fence is built extending from the existing structures to form an enclosure. Such settlements were easily defended and could not be readily burned out by raiders, but they are much work to erect, and some Kaguru consider them uncomfortable because of their lowness, which is required due to the limitations of the building materials used. Today these *tembe*-type structures are found mainly in the west and mountain areas, partly because the mountains are the most conservative area least affected by modern change and partly because the west, though subject to as many changes as the rest of Kaguruland, lacks the ready supply of grass and palms needed for other types of housing. These are the areas with greatest holdings in livestock and thus the most sensitive to the potential dangers of stock theft, which is far less easy to carry out from such palisaded enclosures. Today almost no such dwellings may be found in the higher central parts of the mountains, heavily forested and secure from raids; there, Kaguru always built traditional beehive-type huts such as are found there even now.

Today there are two equally popular alternatives to the *tembe*. One is a rectangular house (*ibanda*) with a series of rooms fronting on a small entry hall; the other is a round beehive-type structure (*musongo*) with two concentric walled spaces with the hearth and sleeping area in the center. Both are made of poles reinforced with plastered, dried earth, and both have thatch roofs. Metal roofs are only attached to rectangular houses. The circular house is said to be the more traditional; more modern-minded Kaguru favor the rectangular house since it allows construction of a series of rooms rather than just two, only one of which is really private. This privacy allows some modern Kaguru to avoid building separate girls' and boys' houses since, with several different rooms with different entries made possible with a rectangular house, little contact need be made between potentially incestuous kin. Often, in such houses, the central hearth around which the traditional circular house is centered is replaced with an outside cooking lean-to patterned after Arab and colonial styles.

The composition of Kaguru settlements follows no particular trend regarding affiliation to kin groups. In the past large settlements were built up around a core matrilineage and persons attached as spouses. Today a few such settlements exist, but only when an elder has acquired considerable wealth and power; the only cases I found involved men who held posts as headmen or chiefs, a few prominent rainmakers and traditional curers, and some very skilled and industrious traders and brewers. Most of the larger settlements are extremely heterogeneous since the persons settled there are attached to nontraditional employers such as a mission, market, or government agency. Smaller settlements are usually composed of kin, but it would be difficult to cite a prevailing pattern; however, among the commoner ones are: (a) a man, his wives, and their married children, especially his married sons and divorced daughters; (b) brothers and their wives and perhaps the brothers' divorced sisters and their children; (c) a man and both his married sons and married nephews; (d) a divorced or widowed woman and her married children with no senior male over them; and (e) a divorced or widowed woman and her daughters, who have various children but who are unmarried and free of direct male control.

# 5

# Marriage, Kin, and Family

THE HOUSEHOLD and the immediate kin relations produced within it (the ties between husband and wife, parents and children, and brothers and sisters) are at the core of Kaguru social relations. The position a person achieves within larger groups, such as a lineage and neighborhood, is grounded in the support secured at the domestic level. One can best explain this by three sets of factors: (1) The household is the basic residential group, containing those persons with whom one most frequently interacts, whose resources, especially food, one shares, and about whom one knows most. It is thought that one can count most on such persons in an emergency. (2) The household is the basic unit of socialization. A child is gradually drawn, through rewards and punishments by his primary kin, into understanding and esteeming the values and goals held by the wider circle of his society. This point is made far clearer in the consideration of Kaguru ritual in Chapter 7. (3) The household is the arena in which many deep loyalties are contested and in which many resources are distributed so that we find that the members of households, including those who later leave the parental nest to set up their own homes, use the loyalties, emotional ties, and moral claims of these original relations as counters in the perpetual game of trying to secure their own individual advantages. The members of a household may each attempt to exploit the values of that group for his or her own ends. These same sentiments which bind persons together within such a group may also be used to drive some apart; adult offspring may be forced during a crisis to choose betwen mother and father, between one sister and another, as part of the politics of kinship, that is, the jostling and jockeying between persons seeking different goals.

This is not, of course, intended to suggest that Kaguru do not feel deep ties of affection and loyalty between kin, for they do. However, enormous pressures are put upon such ties, and intense competition occurs within the field of primary kin relations precisely because kinship is so deeply important since it provides the basic avenue to broader economic, social, and political security. In any society where kinship is this important, we may be sure that it is a sphere not only of intense sentiment and moral obligations but also, at least potentially, of bitter competition and feelings of betrayal and enmity. Any clear and bright patch of moral directives always implies a corresponding shadowy area of guilt and notions of sin. Kaguru sometimes say that one should and must trust kin before others. Kin, especially matrikin, are thought most unlikely to be witches; yet Kaguru go on to say that the most terrible and dangerous witches of all would-be matrikin, and some admit that such cases of witchcraft have been reported. They are saying that betrayals by kin can and do occur, and when they do, they are occasions of the bitterest acrimony. One can only feel profoundly betrayed by those upon whom one has trusted and counted, and the greater the initial dependence and expectation, the bitterer the sense of betrayal and loss.

The best way to approach this problem of understanding Kaguru primary kin relations is to present a brief, somewhat formalized picture of how different Kaguru view a marriage and the social relations created by the family it produces. In the course of that exposition we shall see contradictions in this general picture since it varies with the point of view of those concerned. This suggests some of the potential lines of conflict in such relations. In the final portion of this chapter, I indicate some of the ways different individuals would gauge their actions and the actions of others, given their particular situations in a family group. I try to illustrate these with some cases of Kaguru social behavior.

## The Strategy of Kaguru Marriage Arrangements

The Kaguru family is an arena or stage in which the members of various social groups attempt to achieve their ends. An entire monograph could be devoted to this problem. Any approach I take here can only provide a rough guide to all the possible variations and intricacies of these relations. A useful way of approaching this problem is to consider the various pressures and attitudes that lead to the marriage of a Kaguru boy and girl. Every Kaguru youth wants eventually to marry since no male is considered wholly adult until he has his own household and children. In any case, men should not draw water, fetch firewood, or prepare food. There are no formal prohibitions against such behavior, but it is seen as demeaning to men; these are women's tasks. Until a youth marries, he depends upon his mother or some other senior kinswoman to do this for him. Furthermore, men should not brew beer, yet beer is required to celebrate any important life crisis and to entertain neighbors who may help one in such chores as building houses and clearing land. Beer is a necessary adjunct to any man's successful social life. A man cannot manage the domestic affairs of life without a wife, and he is therefore subordinated to the routines and schedules of another household, his father's or uncle's, until he himself is married. In the past Kaguru youths began to press their elders for wealth to secure a wife within a few years after their initiation. Of course, bachelorhood has its pleasures for Kaguru, and a few youths postpone marriage until their late twenties so that they can fully savor the joys of drinking at clubs, seducing girls at dances and beer clubs, and traveling about in the dry season. However, such pleasures are not wholly abandoned even after marriage. Today a few youths postpone marriage far longer than in the past in order to complete higher education. Those few educated men with no wives who are stationed in Kaguruland on government or mission service have a difficult time since they are viewed with suspicion by their fellows. They require female aid for chores and cooking if they are to maintain respect in Kaguru eyes, yet their salaries are such as to make them unfair competitors with local men seeking women's favors.

In the past a young man depended upon the economic and political aid of his elder kin to help him secure his first wife. Youths worked diligently for such men with the promise of help if they conformed. The problem of securing a wife provided one of the ways by which younger men were tied in dependence to their elders. Among Kaguru, elders manipulated their juniors primarily through the fact that not only did these elders control the young women required by youths but they also controlled the wealth by which these women could be secured. Youths were thereby tied to those kin groups which had provided wealth for them. Today some Kaguru youths, especially those with education, secure their own bridewealth with relatively little direct aid from their kin, although even in such cases, the support they received during their education still may oblige them to their kin. A youth goes into his first marriage hoping to establish his own household and, through a wife and children, hoping to improve his economic and social situation. His aim at the beginning is to marry while incurring as few constricting obligations as possible to those who help him secure a wife. If he takes other wives later, these will be secured from wealth acquired through his own labor and good fortune and no such obligations are likely to be incurred.

A girl's views on marriage are different. She is more fully under the control of her elders, usually her father and her mother's elder kinsmen, who have led her to expect to be married shortly after she has been initiated at puberty. In the past, when there was less communication between different areas of Kaguruland and polygyny was more common, women were scarcer for youths, and some girls were promised in marriage while still children or even before they were born. Girls are often given in their first marriage while quite young, in their late teens or early twenties, and such women make far less mature and shrewd assessments of their situations than their mates. The situation changes profoundly with time, in the case of older women, widows, divorcees, and those few independent souls who resent control by men. Most girls dislike leaving home, and some approach marriage with considerable uneasiness about what their husbands will expect of them. Nonetheless, nearly all girls realize that children are the major source of prestige, influence, and security for them. However, it is obvious that a woman need not be married to bear children. She secures some advantages by having a husband, but disadvantages are entailed in marriage as well, for a husband tries to control as many of his wife's activities as he can.

The formal rules of Kaguru society support male authority and discourage formal indoctrination of a girl into the details of jural rules. Kaguru never say that a woman marries (kutola); she is always married (kutolwa, the passive form). Marriage is something arranged by men as the outcome of male goals. But women learn quickly, and the shy and pliable young bride sometimes becomes a tough and clever older woman quite the match for any man. The reader must remember, however, that all this discussion of social manipulation and potential tensions does not mean that many Kaguru marriages are not happy affairs with consider-

*A Kaguru girl.*

able affection. But marriages are not usually contracted with these feelings as the primary goals or motives, and other factors encourage what Kaguru claim is a fairly high divorce rate.

As a woman matures, she more fully grasps the fact that her primary security lies in children even more than in having a husband, who may indeed restrict her freedom. It is hardly surprising that today, with no threat of raiding, many Kaguru widows and divorcees live alone but continue to bear children by various lovers. Despite its drawbacks, many women seem to judge this arrangement more to their advantage than further marriages. The initial marriage provides experience and other opportunities for women to break somewhat free of their kin so that such an independent life is made possible.

Given that, traditionally at least, both girls and boys want to get married fairly soon after their initiation, what factors determine the ease with which they enter marriage, and what do these factors involve in terms of the subsequent life of these persons? In general, Kaguru boys face far more difficulties than girls in marrying. Most Kaguru girls are disposable in marriage, even those considered ugly or subnormal in intelligence. Of course, a poorly endowed girl commands lower bridewealth than an attractive, healthy girl, but such is the desire for wives and children that any woman may find a husband if she wants. One might say that it is a "seller's market" since men must provide some wealth or services to legitimize their access to women and secure rights over their children, and since polygyny is still practiced.

A youth's ease in entering marriage depends upon a complex set of factors. To begin with, sons are provided with bridewealth in order of birth. A youth must usually wait until all of his elder brothers have married before he may. Furthermore, bridewealth, which ranges today from about $30–50 (200–350 shillings), represents a considerable sum and cannot always be easily secured. If a youth has many sisters near him in age, he may hope that the bridewealth received from some of them may go for his own marriage. A youth with many sisters and few brothers is at a decided advantage. Sometimes brothers will be assigned different sisters on whose bridewealth they can count. A selfish father or uncle may try to use such wealth to make an additional marriage for himself, though he then risks losing a youth's loyalty. Younger sons may therefore wait long before marriage, especially if they have few sisters or if their fathers and uncles are poor. As a consequence, in poorer households youths may move off to seek the support of other kin.

Thinking in terms of modern western European customs, we sometimes entertain the illusion that marriages in other societies are made according to the aims of the couple involved, yet this is rarely so. Among Kaguru, a marriage is the result of the manipulations by two sets of adults, the girl's kin and the boy's. The views of the boy and girl involved are taken into account, but these are not usually considered of primary importance. The boy's position is most problematical. A Kaguru marriage may be seen as the outcome of a struggle to decide the residence of the groom, a struggle determined by the youth's vulnerability to the controls of his elders, though every youth would like to be master of his own fate and reside wherever he desires.

Considering this, the aims of the young men and women who marry must be considered in terms of the strategies employed by their elders. For an elder, the marriage of someone over whom he has control presents several alternatives: He may consolidate his control of a youth by contributing heavily to the bridewealth with the understanding that the youth resides with him or may keep control of a girl by giving her to a youth in exchange for little payment but with the stipulation that the youth move into the new wife's (the elder's) village. Then the elder has gained a follower whom he can control, but at a cost. This assumption of debt may take several forms. The most common would be that the youth's father would make payments with the expectation that his son, in response to his father's paternal concern, would build a new house near him to be a help to his father in his old age. In cases where a father is poor or where he has quarreled with his son, or where an impatient youth is the youngest of a long line of sons awaiting matrimonial aid, a youth might seek the help of other kin. This would usually be an elder in the youth's matrilineage, the kin group in competition with his father for the loyalty of that youth. To explain the dynamics of this competition and also the ways by which elders use their kin connections to win the loyalty of youths, I must digress briefly into a description of how Kaguru lineages resemble credit banks which grant loans and extend credit.

In each Kaguru lineage there are a few elderly men who are recognized as holding legal authority over the women and junior men of that group. In a sense these men are in competition for power, but their individual strength exists only as a result of their cooperation with one another. For example, it is true that a set of brothers may compete for the loyalty of their sisters and these sisters' children, but these men may in turn come to one another's assistance, especially in situations where this does not involve power within the lineage, namely, where each man is attempting to assert control over his own children, who are not members of that man's own lineage. There are two ways in which these men may cooperate. They may loan one another cash or livestock with which the receiver will pay bridewealth for himself or his kin. These loans must be repaid, either by the elder or by the youth who benefitted.

However, there is another way that elders cooperate, which has far more complex repercussions in terms of Kaguru lineage affairs. A Kaguru elder may give a girl from his lineage to a related youth, perhaps even to his own son, with the understanding that the youth resides near him. The lineage gains control of an additional man while not losing control, even temporarily, of the girl. This is said to have been a very common practice in the past, when matrilineages were far stronger and even the most independently minded youths had to reside with some kin group and could not, as now, safely set up homesteads apart from others. In such cases, while the lineage gained control over persons, some individuals within the lineage lost bridewealth. The main reason a youth would be willing to bear the disadvantage of residing with his wife's kin would be because he lacked sufficient wealth to secure a wife on his own terms. If no such wealth were forthcoming from the youth, the girl's kin would lose wealth on the marriage. The wealth gained by a lineage from the marriage of one of its girls is shared between a number of the lineage's members, yet the youth and girl can only reside in one place and can thus only benefit a few of the persons within the lineage. Thus, the elder who gains most from such a marriage has, in a sense, put himself into debt with many of his fellows who have endured some loss but have not reaped any corresponding gain. The members of a lineage hope to resolve this with the arrangements of subsequent marriages. As a result, the allocation of wealth received for any girl represents a complex and tangled history of previous marriages. If there had been no previous marriages in a kin group (an impossible and only hypothetical situation), wealth would be distributed to the seniormost, close relative in the girl's lineage, namely, her mother's oldest brother or, were all such men dead, the girl's eldest brother; if such brothers were unavailable, then the next nearest maternal relative, say, the girl's mother's sister's son, and so on. However, nothing is so simple. Because men may have several sisters, not to mention other junior women in their lineage, they and their predecessors have set up debts of obligations due to the peculiar distribution of wealth from previous marriages. For this reason Kaguru sometimes say that the debts established at a woman's marriage are only repaid at the marriage of her daughter or daughter's daughter, when further wealth comes into the lineage for further redistribution.

Marriages generate a sequence of unique but related networks of debt and obligation between a wide range of kinsmen. Bridewealth debts express the corporate or perpetual character of Kaguru kin groups, for debts continue beyond the life span of an individual. In this sense, a Kaguru lineage may be called corporate, for its life span is like a corporation, a body unto itself, with a life span independent of any of the persons who happen to make up that group at any time.

These are the rules in the case of wealth gained from the marriage of a girl within a lineage. Kaguru say that in the past most of the wealth received in marriage went to the lineage. Furthermore, they add that in the past such payments were usually low because the lineage rarely gave up such a girl, the youth generally being required either to reside with his wife's group or to visit her periodically while he himself stayed on with his own kin; only elderly, rich men took their wives away from their villages. Whatever the truth of these assertions by Kaguru about their past, this is hardly the case today. Considerable wealth is still paid to a girl's lineage, but usually between two-thirds and three-fifths of bridewealth is now paid to the girl's father or, if he is dead, to his closest lineal kinsman. Some Kaguru say that, theoretically, a man may do as he pleases with such wealth, even putting it aside to secure a new wife for himself. However, in practice this wealth is usually distributed to many of the father's own lineal kin. Sometimes this goes toward paying off other debts which the father has accumulated through previous marriage arrangements. Sometimes it goes toward the marriage of one of his sons; this case still indirectly benefits the father since the wealth works toward putting his son in obligation to him. Kaguru provide two explanations for these changes in the payment of bridewealth. They say that bridewealth payments have risen enormously during the colonial period because men can no longer force young affines to live in their bride's villages and work so that any material advantage to be gained from marrying off a girl must be realized immediately through a payment. They also explain the larger portion of wealth given a girl's father by saying that a father only receives wealth once for a marriage, whereas a lineage gains perpetual wealth from a marriage, first through the bride, then through her daughters' marriages, then through these women's daughters' marriages, and so on. More sociological explanations relate to the decline in the lineage as a political and residential unit due to political changes.

About a quarter of Kaguru marriages are made between related kin as arranged by certain elders who thereby manage to control juniors through the form of residence these youths must thereby adopt. From the point of view of a youth, these arrangements may take two forms: (1) He may marry a daughter of one of the men of his lineage. Anthropologists sometimes call this mother's brother's daughter marriage (or matrilateral cross-cousin marriage), though this only rarely involves the actual daughter of one's actual mother's brother—at least among the Kaguru. In this case, the youth often resides with the bride's father or must secure the approval of the lineage elders who made the marriage arrangements as to where he sets up his first homestead, at least during the early years of the marriage. (2) The youth may marry a girl from his father's lineage. This is sometimes called father's sister's daughter marriage (or patrilateral cross-cousin marriage), though among the Kaguru this too only very rarely involves an immediate relative. In such a marriage, the boy's father has especially strong control of the youth and of the youth's children, who will be of their paternal grand-father's lineage and not, of course, of the father's.

In both cases, the residence pattern is of considerable disadvantage to the youth, for he is under the direct control of a kin group to whom he is in debt and to whom his wife can appeal on her own right. In the second case, he is in a particularly weak position toward his own children since the major persons with whom he must contend for his children's loyalties—the members of their lineage —reside with him, his wife, and his children. Such forms of marriage have been called "preferential" by some social anthropologists, but it should be remembered that this adjective can hardly refer to the attitude of the youth, who is generally conceded by Kaguru to have been at some disadvantage in his circumstances ever to embark upon such a union in the first place. Whatever preferences were involved refer to those of elders who gained, or at least hoped to gain, from the match. There are other forms of such "preferential marriages" among the Kaguru; however, the principles of strategy remain similar.[1]

Both boys and girls have ways of circumventing these arrangements by their elders. A boy might elope with a willing girl, but in the past he risked being killed if caught. Elopement is fairly safe today, but he may still risk fines through a court. Another tactic is to get a girl pregnant. The pregnancy is seen as a measure of the intractable defiance of the couple, and realistic parents often give in to the marriage. Furthermore, if a girl is pregnant, she is, at least until the child is weaned, undesirable to others, so that her parents sometimes accept less favorable terms from the suitor available than they might otherwise do. These are risky ventures, however, and only desperate boys with poor prospects, very strong-willed girls, or those deeply in love would so vex their kin.

However, no one may marry just anyone. Marriage within one's own clan is impossible; for Kaguru this is tantamount to witchcraft. Although sexual rela-tions within one's clan are spoken of in horror, many Kaguru tales and legends deal with this theme. One may not marry anyone whose father has the same clan as one's own father. It is said that this is so because it would place such men in opposition to one another, both in the arrangements over bridewealth and in the loyalties toward their children, whereas such men should support and help one another as members of one clan. Kaguru expect kin of different lineages to be involved in competitive roles (as in the cousin marriage mentioned previously), but they do not expect this of kin of the same clan or lineage. It may happen that very distantly related kin wish to marry; sometimes this is allowed after a cere-mony which symbolically wipes out kin ties. Some Kaguru say that this may account for the fact that certain clans have similar names.

Kaguru also insist that no men of the same clan should have wives from the same clan. The worst instance of this would be a polygynous man who had taken sisters as wives, but brothers and cousins within the same lineage also should never marry women of the same clan. Since some clans may number over a thousand persons scattered over a very wide distance, some of whom do not see or know one another, this rule is not observed literally, but men of the same lineage or distantly related men living near one another conform. Kaguru say that

---

[1] These marriages are discussed further elsewhere (Beidelman 1966).

this rule prevents kinswomen from becoming sexual competitors for the same men, for this would disrupt the warm feelings which should exist between clans-women. While Kaguru consider this obvious and commonsensical, we should remember that some other matrilineal peoples, such as the Navajo, reason quite differently and consider such marriages to sisters ideal for preserving harmony between women.

However, affairs between such prohibited partners do take place from time to time. These relations are thought to cause serious illness among the kin of both offenders. This can only be averted through confession and treatment by the joking partners of the couple concerned, who undertake rites to remove the pollution.

## The Form of Households

Kaguru say that every man, at least every pagan man, would like as many wives as possible. It is quite common for persons to have had several spouses over the years. It is also said that in the past many men had more than one wife, whereas now this is no longer common. Today in the highly acculterated areas where there is considerable education, higher incomes, and greater aspiration to European and Christian customs about 6 percent of the married women are part of some polygynous, extended household; in the more remote, traditional areas about 18 percent are.

A Kaguru household may be seen as a group organized around the production and allocation of resources, the basic resources being foodstuffs, craft objects, and human offspring. These common concerns both unite and divide the members of this group. Each woman has her own fields, chickens, and gardens which she tends. She may also make some income through brewing and selling beer and making mats, baskets, or pottery, which she may sell to her neighbors or at a local market. Many wives buy and sell goods at markets with a fairly free hand, but this is at the discretion of their husbands. By tradition, a wife has no legal right to dispose of any goods without the approval and knowledge of her husband. However, a husband's control over his wife is tied to various obligations. He must provide food and care for his wife, even when she is continuously ill and cannot care for herself, and he should purchase basic items, such as cloth, blankets, and utensils, which she needs. Besides the fields and gardens which a woman or her children work for their own needs, they should all work at least some of the time on fields belonging to the head of the household. The produce from these fields may be used by the household head as he sees fit. Similarly, if the father owns a herd of sheep or goats, he may dispose of these as he wishes, though if he allots certain animals to his wife and children, he cannot take them back to use in any way he wishes. He must justify such acts. A man's dependents produce two kinds of assets: those which go for their own well-being and support, and which he can control only in a limited sense, and those which he controls outright. Thus, a man with several wives would not take foodstuffs from one wife and sell them to provide a gift for another. However, he is obliged to dip into his own wealth to provide a minimum standard of living for all his wives. If he finds wealth for a

*A Kaguru husband and wife.*

third wife, it would be from his own personal resources held in a granary and herd kept independently of his present wives.

It is said that a husband should get the permission of his present wives before taking any additional wives, but this is not always done. Co-wives seem somewhat jealous of one another, and Kaguru tell many stories about the witchcraft practiced between co-wives and about the bitter feeling and rivalries between a man's children by different women. Nonetheless, many polygynous households seem to run smoothly with wives cooperating in household chores. Some Kaguru say that the worst disaster to befall a man would be if he had two wives who conspired together against him. Some cynics say that the ideal arrangement would be three wives, for while two might be in league, the third almost always would be at odds with the other two and thus would inform on them to her husband. So long as all the various wives bear children and are healthy, polygynous households seem to work fairly well, but where one wife lacks children while another has several, odds are high that the infertile wife will blame the fertile one as a witch causing sterility.

## The End of Marriage: Death and Divorce

If a woman dies, no bridewealth is refunded to her husband; it is just bad luck. If the groups united by a marriage consider it desirable to perpetuate this relationship, a kinswoman of the dead woman, perhaps even her sister, may be substituted with only a token additional payment. This is said to be done because the two groups of affines like being related. It is easy to see the advantages to this in the case of marriage with a chief, rainmaker, or rich man. If the husband has other wives, these may be asked to serve as stepmothers to orphaned children. The wealth allocated to the original mother's household should be kept for her children and not mixed with that of any other wife, but inroads on wealth are common where the children are young and the husband strongly influenced by the surviving wife. In the case of divorce, children may temporarily go with the mother, especially if they are young and being nursed. It is said that once the children are mature, the true legal claims will be made. A father will arrive to demand his share of any bridewealth gained from his daughter's marriage, and a grown son begins to visit his father in search of bridewealth for his first wife.

If her husband dies, a woman is urged to remain with her dead husband's kin. These maintain that they had all helped pay for her marriage and that she should therefore be taken by another in the deceased's lineage. In the past a woman would be forced into widow inheritance (*uhasa*); today widows can refuse, and indeed most do, often setting themselves up as independent house-holders only loosely connected with their kin. This is especially likely if they have already borne some children.

For Kaguru divorce is a more socially complex marital problem than death. In general, men rarely desire a divorce and do all they can to prolong and frustrate litigation. A wife must be exceedingly quarrelsome and difficult before a husband seeks a separation. This is because the Kaguru method of bridewealth refund at divorce rarely favors a husband. Where the marriage is childless or where the husband holds a high political post or is rich, a girl's relatives are loath to agree to a divorce, even when the man's conduct has been judged wrong by general standards. Ironically, the more children a woman has borne, the more her kin gain materially from her divorce. They are allowed to deduct 50 or 60 shillings from bridewealth for each child the woman has produced, even if the children did not survive. Thus, a girl could marry at the age of sixteen, bear five or six children, seek a divorce, and still be in her late twenties and easily marriageable to another husband. Even if the original bridewealth was 300 to 400 shillings (a high amount), her kin would not be obliged to return more than a token payment of a few shillings. At divorce the wife keeps all that her husband gave her as well as those goods produced from her gardens. A woman might well take some of her younger children with her. It is her husband, therefore, who is the real loser, having to raise new bridewealth payments for another wife and having to worry about the disloyalty and suspicion his wife and her kin might sow in the minds of his younger children, who have moved with her.

The interests of all involved change as a marriage endures. Paradoxically, the longer a couple are married, if they bear children, the greater the advantages the wife and her kin may derive from a divorce. Of course, this discounts the fact that the longer a couple remain together, the more likely they will find things which hold them together in terms of sentiment and daily customary attachments.

## Children and Marriage

The real complication in domestic social relations only arises with the birth of children. Until then, most Kaguru marriage are not considered complete and neither spouse is permanently attached to the other's group. With children, however, a person is connected through them to his spouse's kin, even after divorce or the death of his mate. A widow may dislike her husband's kin and move off to live independently of his or even her kin; but when one of her sons matures and needs help in securing wealth to marry, she and her son will remonstrate with both his sets of kin for aid. The logistics of most Kaguru kin relations depend on the interplay of three sets of loyalties: those toward one's own household, those toward one's maternal kin, and those toward one's father's kin. As we have seen, the quality of this interplay varies through time. Until marriage, an individual judges his advantages simply in terms of maximizing benefits from both paternal and maternal kin. After a marriage the situation changes profoundly since one retains these loyalties but must now balance these off against other ties and interests. Once a man sets up his own household, he no longer sees the interests of his parental group as being so close to his own. He must sometimes humor his wife and provide for her welfare and comfort if she is to remain loyal and helpful. Correspondingly, a wife can, if she is lucky, gain some freedom and independence through marriage. After all, she will then have her own house to run and, barring a meddlesome mother-in-law, she can use her husband's affections and needs as the reason for a growing lack of involvement in her parental group. Where a Kaguru husband and wife find affection and compatibility, such manipulation becomes part of the general give and take of domestic affairs. Where marriage are unhappy, this provides recognized grounds for divorce.

A husband and wife are both united in their concern for their children, and both tend to see offspring as their solace and protection in old age. However, a father and mother are tied very differently to their children. Kaguru say that fathers love their children, especially their sons, but that fathers cannot do all that they would like for their children. This is because a father belongs to a different clan and lineage from that of his children; to the extent that he remains loyal and true to his fellow lineage mates and their demands, he cannot help his own children. In contrast, a Kaguru mother has no ties which take precedence over those to her children. Of course, she has conflicting ties, such as those toward her own parents, her husband, and her brothers, but none of these is expected to be maintained to the extent that it would prejudice her children's best interests. A Kaguru man is caught in the crosscurrents of conflicting jural obligations to the

*Kaguru women braiding hair.*

members of his lineage and the members of his household; this is the price he pays for enjoying formal authority in a matrilineal system. A Kaguru mother has no such involvement with authority and, consequently, equates her aspirations with her offspring's. Thus, she is seen by her children as the surest expositor of their own interests. The mother-child bond is the most important and valued tie in Kaguru society. Although Kaguru describe this relationship in somewhat idyllic, even altruistic, terms, it is colored by the tone of authority and power relations. Some Kaguru women use their children's loyalties to gain influence and power, even at the expense of their children's own welfare; furthermore, even when women believe themselves devoted to their children's best interests, they may still order these children (for their own good) to act in ways which will secure the help and protection of elders.

These complexities become clearer when we see the implications which mother-child ties can have when they are projected through time, when a couple's children have borne children. At this point the unproblematical and "pure" feelings of mothers and children may be used in the varying efforts by some to control others within a matrilineage.

In a Kaguru lineage, authority is held by a senior male [*bulai* (mother's brother)] over juniors of his generation and over the children of his kinswomen. This authority is sustained by the pressures of self-interest upon various elders, determined in part by common values of lineage loyalty and ancestral respect held by all lineage members and in part by dependence which the poorer, less socially adroit persons have upon elders for help and guidance. Underlying these are deep, complex affectual bonds between children and their mothers. This is shown by the fact that men and women rarely repudiate and ignore their elders while their own mother lives, whereas many Kaguru begin to present their own interests, as opposed to the elders', once their mother is dead. Once their mother is dead, men attempt to head their own lineage segments, brothers often breaking with brothers, and men often break from the authority of their mother's brothers when the woman joining them, the mother's brother's mother, is gone.[2] A simple diagram should clarify this:

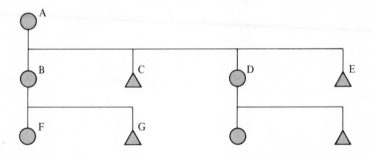

C is the leading elder of the lineage members shown here. All members are descended from A, their common ancestress. Were A's husband dead, C would be wise to invite her to reside with him. C is the eldest son of A and attempts to control both his younger brother E and his two sisters, B and D, as well as their children. To varying degrees, all these persons would really like to be independent of C. The main obstruction is the tie which each person feels toward A. All of the elder persons are brothers and sisters, children of A. The inforcement of sibling ties through maternal ties tend to hold such kin together. From A's point of view, her greatest social prestige and power depend on her double role both as mother to many children and as the future ancestress of what may one day be a large matrilineage. An elderly woman usually exerts every effort to secure the continued cooperation between her children and their children in turn. She acts out of her desire for social esteem and power and her hope for some kind of immortality in being remembered by her descendants in their prayers to the dead, as well as out of a genuine desire that her children remain morally one. She does this by playing upon the sentiments and feelings of her children. In part this

---

[2] I discuss this situation in considerable detail elsewhere ("Further Readings, The Kaguru," Beidelman 1961a).

attachment is due to the manner in which Kaguru children are raised with a prolonged and close relation between mother and child, even after subsequent children are born. The attachment is probably also the result of Kaguru values, that is, the mother-child relation is constantly proclaimed the most valued relation, and so persons try to demonstrate such affection, perhaps even when these emotions may not be quite so keenly felt as the actors maintain. A Kaguru proverb says, "Mother is god [in his gentle, kind aspect]."

Another way of considering these relations is to see a mother as the center of a communication network. She is the only person by whom all those pictured on the diagram may interrelate with one another. Through visits she becomes a relay point for news and a pivot for influencing the various members into taking certain action. E may well wish to control some of his sisters, their bridewealth, and children and resent C's primacy; however, if C has A's support, he will probably be able to dominate all of his fellow siblings and their children. Each of A's daughters will one day occupy a position similar to A's; each will also become an elderly woman with her own incipient subordinate lineage. What stops such a woman from asserting herself (in the purported interest of her sons and daughters) is the force of the moral and sentimental tie to her own mother, who tells her, by words and acts, "You must give in to your brother; I, your mother, tell you to do so!" When A dies, C and E may struggle over the future allegiance of their sisters (B and D). Once A is dead, C's power is diminished along another front. Previously, C might admonish B to urge her children to conform, and A would reinforce his views by insisting upon the importance of brothers and sisters standing together; but once A is dead, no such moral force is available. With A's death C's power is threatened, and it is likely that E will split off from him; even G may insist on his own future. Yet there is no mother to preach harmony and reconciliation. Moreover, each sister sees this division as her opportunity to head her own group, to fill the same role as A herself filled. Within the pattern of any mother-child relation we can predict two sets of disparate, even antagonistic relationships. Loyalties corrode in the acid of time. The force of maternal ties which hold A to B, C, D, and E will split these apart when A dies because the maternal ties of B and D lead each of these sisters to promote her own children, probably through the sponsorship of a particular brother. Parochial solidarity toward one mother leads to sororal separatism within a matrilineal system.

It should be obvious by now how widowhood accentuates the prowess of women. Motherhood of mature children in a matrilineal society provides a means for social advance; how much more useful if the woman's role is not impeded by the controls set by a husband and father of her children.

This prowess is modified from situation to situation, depending upon the case; what is important is an appreciation of the values applied in each situation. Motherhood is the ultimate sacred value among Kaguru, yet it is only by the death of certain women (for example, one's mother's mother) that a man advances his position within a lineage. This is a sociological truth which is highly objectionable to those Kaguru who are asked about its significance. The reasons for their distaste is obvious.[3]

---

[3] For those to whom this is not obvious, see Beidelman 1966 and "Further Readings, Kaguru," Beidelman 1951a.

Kaguru men have a profound interest in the fertility and sexual desirability not only of their own wives but also of their daughters and sisters, women to whom they are forbidden sexual access. The relation between brother and sister is the most ambiguous in Kaguru society. A brother is keenly absorbed in the fertility of his sisters since they furnish him with heirs, but customary etiquette prohibits any sexual allusions or sexually toned acts in the company of siblings of either sex. Kaguru folklore and jokes abound which indicate tensely emotional but ambivalent feelings between brothers and sisters.

The broad principles of Kaguru kin relations derive from ties set out in my discussion of domestic (household) and lineal relations. However, two ties deserve at least brief mention: those between members of alternate generations of kin and those between cross-cousins. The first depends upon the principle: My enemy's enemy is my friend. Every parent is both an obedient child (the first in a series of followers to his own parent's group) and a rebellious founder of a kin group to which he will attempt to subordinate his own offspring. In a game for power and loyalties an ambitious man's parents and children share common interest in keeping him in check. Kaguru custom abounds in wordplay, etiquette, and reciprocal kindnesses thought to reflect these common interests between grandparents and grandchildren.

Kaguru marry cross-cousins, which fits in with their notion of marrying persons toward whom they have some tense, otherwise unresovable and problematical relation. The source of this tension is the conflict over inheritance manifested in Kaguru society through contradictory commitments to both lineal and household principles. Cross-cousins then become competitors for wealth, in terms of inheritance and in terms of the favors an elder (their father's/mother's brother) dispenses from day to day. A man, as a good father, will be urged by his wife and children to give them all he can of his resources, while his sister (and probably his mother) will urge him to help her children, his future lineal heirs. Both groups have strong claims upon him, and he would like to please them both. No matter how fairly he tries to act, some are likely to feel slighted. The main affectual pressures on a man come from women; his mother and sister emphasize his lineal loyalties, his wife his domestic ones. It is easy for Kaguru to view the women of their father's lineage, especially their father's sisters, as inimical. Kaguru say that one marries enemies to convert them into friends, and it should surprise no one to learn that all women of one's father's lineage and clan, including his sisters, are potential wives (Beidelman 1966).

The issues raised in this chapter are complex. There is no clear answer to all the problems presented, but the discussion, together with the cases presented here, illustrate some of the factors ordering Kaguru kin relations. Each case illustrates some important factors discussed previously. The reader should have little trouble recognizing the basic social processes exhibited in each and can ponder them in terms of the possible long-term course these affairs might take.

a. Tomasi's Case

Tomasi was an orphan. He lacked immediate kin to provide bridewealth for a wife. Tomasi's mother was a lineal kinswoman to a subchief. This maternal uncle provided Tomasi with a wife, a girl of this subchief's father's lineage. Tomasi's uncle made arrangements so that the ordinary bridewealth was avoided by Tomasi, while the uncle payed off some of the relatives himself. As recompense, however, Tomasi had to move into his new wife's village, that of her parents and his uncle. There, he was expected to provide extra labor for these kin who, in this case, were also his affines. Tomasi sometimes drank, and when he did, he spoke bitterly of his lot as a mere servant among his own kin. One day while drunk he attacked his wife and affines with a knife; later he was forced into abject public apologies with the alternative that if he did not, he would be divorced by his wife. His uncle told him that he could easily be divorced since he had paid no proper bridewealth and that they would keep the children. Tomasi could then hunt on his own for wealth for a new wife. Tomasi stayed on, unhappy.

b.   Maria's Case

Maria was the daughter of Emma, a widowed woman who had left her dead husband's kin and returned to live with members of her matrilineage, in this case, a subchief. Emma brought with her not only Maria but also a son, who married and resided in this same village. Her elder, a chiefly kinsman, was pleased to have three new households added to his village and was careful to flatter and encourage his new clients so that they did not return to the dead man's village. Maria's mother was an elderly, clever, aggressive woman and tried to encourage the same traits in her daughter. Maria had a son by an unknown lover; later she married a messenger from the subchief's court and her kin, including the subchief, gained bridewealth. The men of Maria's lineage had a strong claim for some of this wealth and so did the men of Maria's father's lineage, but the major part of this wealth as well as the general arrangements about the choice of a mate and where they would live were made as Emma wanted. Maria now resides only 10-minute walk from Emma, and they both continue to lead free lives, brewing beer and entertaining men.

c.   Anna's Case

Anna was born out of wedlock. No one recognized any father for her. It was not simply that her mother's lover refused to pay wealth to legitimize his fathered child; rather, no one was even able to determine who the father might be; Anna's mother would not tell. Anna grew up in her parent's village. She had a matrilineage but no father's kin. She began early to brew beer and take lovers. She now has several children by different lovers and has not disclosed the lovers' names. The children, like herself, belong only to her own lineage and lack paternal kin. Anna's lineage has lost much on account of this behavior in that no bride-wealth has been gained for Anna (nor for her mother) and no new kin ties were generated by giving her in marriage to another group. However, Anna's lineage, along with Anna's mother's father, holds uncontested legal and moral control over Anna and Anna's children. Anna herself told me that she was sad in some ways that she was not married and that she had no husband or father to whom to appeal when she felt that her own matrikin were neglecting her. She had no group to pit against them in competition for her loyalty. Her legal security was in the hands of her natal kin, on whom she therefore depended unduly. Although what cash she made through brewing and lovers was her own, she had no husband from whom to demand clothing and other goods as her right. Her kin looked forward to the maturation of Anna's daughters, for they would secure all the bridewealth gained by these girls' marriages and thereby regain the wealth they considered lost through the failure of Anna's mother to declare a lover and Anna's own stubborness in the same respect. Anna had gained considerable personal freedom, but at a price.

### d. Yeremia's Case

Yeremia's wife has had tuberculosis for many years. Yeremia has spent considerable money treating his wife, who remains ill and away in a hospital. Yeremia has no help in cooking and working in the fields. Furthermore, his wife seems unlikely to bear any more healthy children. Yeremia and his wife are Christians and the C.M.S. mission rarely grants divorce. Yeremia has now begun arrangements to secure a second wife. He acknowledges that it would be wrong to abandon his first wife in her troubles, but he misses a bed partner and wants more children and help in his fields. He has chosen a young, pagan girl unlikely to object to the unchristian side of the marriage. He has avoided telling his wife, who is still away in the hospital. When she comes home, she will find a new co-wife in a newly erected house nearby.

### e. Musa's Case

Musa is often the butt of his friends' jokes. He is unpopular and quarrelsome and a well-known thief. Although handsome and young, when drunk he confesses that he has very unsatisfactory sexual relations with women. He is not considered a desirable match for a girl. An elder of his lineage, in whose settlement he lives, made Musa marry Musa's dead brother's widow, for which the lineage had already paid bridewealth. The widow had already borne a child for Musa's dead brother. Musa was not very happy with the marriage and was said to have proved an unsatisfactory lover. His new wife carried on a flagrant, adulterous affair with another man for whom she bore a child. Musa secured an adultery fine from the man but kept the child and did not divorce the wife. She has now borne a third child, and neighbors wonder who the real father may be. Musa and his wife often quarrel, and Musa is often away from home drunk. His wife is an aggressive woman and shows little inclination to leave her husband.

### f. Jakson's Case

Jakson is an orphan. He married a girl after paying very little bridewealth and built a homestead about 10-minutes walk from his wife's father, a famous curer and diviner. His wife's kin continually interfered with his domestic affairs. Jakson and his wife had a son who was not well tended by the wife. Jakson had sufficient education to press for his son to be treated at the local mission clinic, where the case was diagnosed as malnutrition. However, the wife insisted that her father treat the child and it finally died. Jakson divorced his wife, but then found himself with little resources to secure a new wife. Jakson is young and considered handsome. He seduced a girl in a more distant village. He refused to confess his guilt until the child was born, claiming that were he to do so, he might be subject to fines were she to die in childbirth. Later, the girl bore a son and Jakson married her and set up a house in a new settlement far from his affines. He paid only a small bridewealth since the girl's parents wanted their "ruined" Christian daughter to be married and respectable.

### g. Munyesi's Case

Ndagila took his wife, Munyesi, and her father, Mukomwa, to court. Here is the court's terse digest of the case:

> Ndagila: I want my wife, who is at her father's house. I sent her there to enjoy Christmas, but now she refuses to return. I also want to complain about this woman and how she behaved when we visited a settlement near Kitete. When we were there, my wife asked me to let her go to a dance but I refused and we quarreled. Later she asked permission to go to the latrine, but she didn't return. When I looked outside I saw her running toward a certain house. When I tried to fetch her from that place, I was beaten up by some people in that house and I had a tooth knocked out. When I went to her father to give him bridewealth, he said that I was not paying enough and that he would not accept what I offered.
>
> Munyesi: This man is not my husband. He is only a boyfriend. He did not marry me because he did not pay any bridewealth at all. What he said is not true.
>
> Mukomwa: My daughter was taken by this man, Ndagila. They lived together for three years, but I never received any bridewealth from him. He gave me a small amount of money when he took her, but that is an adultery fine.

Ndagili is in a weak position regarding the bridewealth he appears to have paid. Had Munyesi remained with him and agreed with his claims, Mukomwa would not be able to dismiss Ndagila's claims so lightly. Once some bridewealth has been paid and a girl is living willingly with a man, a court tends to try to maintain the marriage and merely tries to force the husband to pay more bridewealth. When I left the field, this case had not yet been settled, but most felt that Ndagila was unlikely to win out against the combined rejections of his wife and her father.

### h. Chitemo and Mugutu

Chitemo married Chifumbe and had two children by her. Then he divorced her and received back his bridewealth. Chifumbe's mother and brother, Mugutu, disliked Chitemo intensely and were pleased with the divorce, especially since they made some profit in the bridewealth involved on account of the deductions made because Chifumbe had borne two daughters. Later Chifumbe regretted the divorce and went back to Chitemo with the consent of neither the mother nor Mugutu and without Chitemo paying bridewealth. She had another child by Chitemo. Mugutu spent many months in court over this case. These difficulties arose because Chifumbe refused to leave Chitemo and return to her mother and brother, who tended to mistreat her. She would run off whenever they tried to take her home forcibly. During the dispute Chitemo is said to have burned down Chifumbe's mother's house; Mugutu attacked Chitemo with his bow and arrows; and both men tried to abduct Chifumbe's children. After many months of litigation in which the case was appealed and retried, Mugutu finally won. None of the expensive and time-consuming litigation or other troubles would have occurred, however, if Chifumbe herself had been a cooperative daughter and sister. If Mugutu had been less quarrelsome and thoughtless, he might have been obeyed by his sister. Had Chitemo been willing to give a bit and pay some bridewealth for Chifumbe, he might have secured her for a relatively small amount. In the end, Chitemo had to pay adultery fines and court fees; but Chifumbe threatens to run away yet again from her kin.

### i. Sambasa's Case

Sambasa keeps running away from her husband's village. Her husband left her to work on the nearby estates, leaving her in the charge of his father. Now Sambasa wants a divorce. At present neither she nor his kin know where her husband is, but his father says that he will provide for Sambasa until his son returns. Sambasa's own father does not want to return the bridewealth he received, especially since Sambasa has borne no children. He strongly criticizes his daughter, and when she runs off, he brings her back to her father-in-law. Sambasa told the court that her father-in-law wants her to stay because he hopes that she will get pregnant by someone in his settlement and that he can then collect adultery fines from any lover she might take. Since neither her own kin nor her husband's kin agreed to the divorce and since she had not been physically mistreated, the court ruled that she had to return to her husband's village.

### j. Joash and Samweli

Here is a case in which a court no longer supports Kaguru tradition since the custom in question is condemned by the government. The court record is as follows:

> Joash: I accuse Samweli of keeping my daughter without having any right to her.
> Samweli: My son married Joash's daughter. Shortly after the marriage my son died. Now this girl should stay with us. We paid wealth for her and by Kaguru custom she is our wife and should live with one of our men.
> Joash: It is bad luck that your boy died. Now I want my daughter back since her husband is gone. This man Samweli is trying to make a prostitute of my daughter. He hopes that if she stays long enough at his village, she will get pregnant. These are modern times and we have learned that such rules are bad. The government does not approve of this.
> Samweli: The girl is already pregnant. You know that a pregnant woman cannot be divorced.

The dispenser from the local clinic was summoned to court and testified that the girl was not pregnant. The court ruled that the girl was to be returned to her kin and that no bridewealth need be refunded.

k. Msulwa's Case

The court record is as follows:

Msulwa: I claim 50 shillings which I loaned to Andrea so that he could marry the daughter of Semgomba. This fellow is my sister's child and he wanted me to help him with this amount which he borrowed. Now I am claiming this amount.

Andrea: Msulwa is my mother's brother and the debt which he says someone owes him may indeed be 50 shillings, but I myself did not borrow it nor do I know if this wife I married was obtained on account of that money. Maybe she knows about this debt. I don't know what arrangements my father made. I myself only know that I have a wife.

Court: Andrea should help Msulwa and should give him the 50 shillings which he claims is owed on account of Andrea's payment of bridewealth for a wife. Msulwa is poor and old and should be helped.

l. Chilimo's Case

Chilimo claimed that Magome owed him one cow as part of the bridewealth which Magome was to pay him for his daughter. Magome admitted that the debt of bridewealth had still not been fully paid, but he claimed that the responsibility for paying it belonged with his son Muga rather than with himself. He told the court, "It is not my concern but his! Let the boy pay! He is sitting here in court. Ask him to pay! It is not my wife but his for whom you are asking that cow!" Magome maintained that he had gained nothing from the marriage despite having helped with the bridewealth payments, for his son had moved away to another settlement. He had expected the youth to live with him because he had helped him, but he and his son had quarreled and the youth had moved off to the village of his mother's brother, Magome's brother-in-law.

The court ruled that Magome had made the original marriage agreement with Chilimo and it was therefore Magome rather than his son Muga who was responsible for completing the payments. However, the court acknowledged that perhaps Muga had been unfair to his father; it suggested that this could be the subject of a future case if Magome wished.

# 6

# Neighborhoods and Chiefs: Political Affairs

## Defining Political Actions

**M**ANY DEFINE political actions as those which involve the legitimate use of power within a particular territory. Such a definition, made famous by Weber, may be useful as a starting point in examining various problems, but it soon becomes clear that such a notion is so oversimplified that if taken no further, it blinds us to the most interesting problems in the study of how people are controlled in society. One way to get at these problems is to examine more carefully the three basic concepts in this definition conveyed by the terms "legitimate," "power," and "territory."

Legitimacy implies the idea that people willingly approve of something; they concede the moral right of those who constrain them. Legitimacy rests upon commonly held ideas and values, but to what extent are such notions actually held by all the members of a society? Legitimate power, which we conveniently term "authority," is sometimes questioned or resented by those over whom it is exerted. This is especially true in a colonial society; the native inhabitants resent the rules imposed by aliens. However, most of the peace and order within a society, its harmony, rests on the fact that the overwhelming majority of the population hold common notions about how to conduct their lives. Men live in accordance with the law even when they are not always aware of its details. This is because the rules of law are merely a reflection of broader, more basic assumptions about the nature of the world and men. These are learned and internalized outside formal legal or political situations. Where this is not so, where the law and political institutions are not closely enmeshed with the other sectors of social life, we may expect a rise both in repressive actions by those in power and in conflict following attempts by those below to elude or manipulate inacceptable rules through illegal or extralegal means. Those benefiting from the situation may call this corruption or lawlessness, but those being exploited see such behavior as the pursuit of reasonable self-interest or as self-defense against an unjust system.

In large, complex societies many different groups interact together, and each such group has its own somewhat different perspective as to who should control others and how this should be done. Furthermore, it is not always easy to separate authority (legitimate power) from power, which is not considered as part of any formal procedure of control such as courts, administrative groups, chiefs, and village meetings. For example, to what extent do Kaguru disobey government rules because they do not regard colonial rule as legitimate?

This leads us to the third term, "territory;" it is not always clear what limits to set to such a unit. For example, when I lived in Kaguruland, many government policies were determined not by the Kaguru within their homeland but by Europeans residing outside that area, some in the colonial administrative centers and some back in Europe. Therefore, any limits I set in constructing an explanatory model must be somewhat arbitrary. Should I consider only a headmanship? A subchiefdom? All of Kaguruland? An administrative district? A province? The entire colony? British colonial policy as determined by conditions back in Britain? A study of political affairs in a colonial situation provides an excellent illustration of the problem of determining just what factors are important in explaining how people are controlled within various social situations.

Before describing the political system of Kaguruland as it existed in the colonial period when I did most of my fieldwork, I should indicate briefly some of the factors that determined its structure during that time. Without an historical background the structure of Kaguru political affairs during this period would seem odd indeed. In colonial times an administration was formed by two opposing cultural principles, one determined by Kaguru tradition and one determined by the force of alien rules and the attitudes and handicaps of those who tried to govern an alien country. The only feature common to all the actors involved, the native Africans and the European administrators alike, was their desire to maximize their own self-interest or that of their group as defined in terms of the values of their particular culture. Europeans took alien values into account only in those areas of life where the cooperation of Africans was essential to their rule.

## The Traditional Political System and Early Colonial Rule

Earlier, I noted that Kaguru clans are associated with various areas which they are thought to own. Thus, in the past Kaguruland was divided into many small, politically autonomous areas; each was dominated by a particular clan, but members of many other clans also lived in these areas. Kaguru themselves tend to speak of this ownership as permanent, but they admit that some clans lost their lands to others. They seem to be suggesting that only so long as a clan was sufficiently strong was it able to make its claims of ownership accepted by others. Thus, while ownership was, in the short term, upheld by conventional values of authority, in the long run, ownership altered with the changing fortunes of groups as these rose or fell in their control of the basic means of power—number, wealth, skillful leadership, and the use of alliances with other such groups. Kaguruland was not traditionally a clear-cut political entity. Various clans exerted influence, but even the most successful controlled only a small part of the area. It was not even true that a common language and customs provided a minimal definition of communality, a kind of moral substratum, for Kaguru at the borders often resembled their tribal neighbors nearly as much as they resembled Kaguru from the opposite side of the Kaguru homeland. Some Kaguru even made temporary alliances with groups clearly alien to the area, such as Baraguyu and Kamba, in order to raid their neighboring fellows.

Kaguru speak of their earlier chiefs, but such a term should not be interpreted in the same sense as the terms "chief" and "ruler" of centralized and stable political groups such as we might associate with parts of West Africa or the Bantu kingdoms of northwest East Africa. Kaguru have two words often translated as chief: *mkulu* and *mundewa*. The first term refers to a senior and important person, a "big" man, and can be applied to anyone from one's elder brother to the head of a court or the most respected man in a neighborhood. The second term relates to the leader of a group; *idewa* means a group, a herd, a flock, or even a cattle enclosure. The term's significance depends on the context in which it is used. An elderly person is likely, due to his seniority, to be the head of some group, but the important leaders would be those men who, through age and the number of their junior kin, through sagacious marriage and other contacts with allied groups, and through shrewdness and intelligence, manage to assert themselves over their neighbors and kin. One is not born to leadership, and even if one attains influence after years of efforts and strategy, it can be undermined and lost if a person loses sight of the factors he has manipulated to reach his eminence. Whenever really difficult disputes or problems arise, it is said that such a leader will always summon all his neighbors and kin and seek their consent before making a decision on what course of action to take; he would not dare voice such a decision in the form of an order. In any case, he would be unable to enforce it without the support of the majority of his followers.

When the first Europeans arrived and set about trying to colonize Kaguruland, they looked for the leaders of the land, assuming that by winning over and coercing such men, they might rule through them. Because of a distorted stereotype they entertained about all African societies having chiefs (perhaps due to the long European contact with West Africa, where such leaders were more common and influential), they seemed to have assumed that Kaguru would have such leaders. When they arrived with guns and gifts and asked the Kaguru for their leaders, one cannot be surprised that some opportunistic local men stepped forward to claim that they had such powers. In any case, such inquiries made political sense, for upstart leaders, claiming more land and followers than any earlier Kaguru had done, were beginning to appear in Kaguruland, and they were potentially useful to any outsiders wishing to rule the country. These men owed their new found powers to the influx of trade goods and weapons into the area through the caravan trade initiated by the Arabs. Their opportunism made them many enemies, and this encouraged their need for arms. They were promoted, first by the Arabs, then by the Germans and British, since they could unite and bring to order far larger groups of Kaguru than had been previously united. Unification is not only a factor allowing people to resist conquest; it may also be introduced to make a people easier to subdue, control, and exploit.

Therefore, when the Germans arrived, they found some Kaguru leaders who with the help of Arabs and African outsiders, had gained control over fairly large areas, stretching even beyond the traditional boundaries of a particular clan. These leaders raided unfriendly neighbors while protecting others from

Arabs and some Africans in return for tribute. The Germans found this practice as useful as had the Arabs, but they preferred to trust coastal Africans rather than unsophisticated upcountry Africans such as the Kaguru. As a consequence, they recognized certain prominent local Kaguru leaders, but they did not pay them any salaries or give them official prerogatives, though they were held responsible if their subjects misbehaved. These men were considered mere local spokesmen for their people. The Germans conveyed their orders through coastal African agents (*akidas*) whom they paid to reside in the area. German rule was brief and harsh, though not as harsh as the anti-German postwar propaganda of the British made it out to be. The *akidas* were unpopular because they had no ties with local people and therefore could not be restrained by those they governed. During this time Kaguru appear to have been only loosely governed. German administrators visited the area mainly during times of crisis, relying otherwise on their African agents. The German administrators were few and the areas they supervised immense. Roads were few and poor, and travel into Kaguruland could be made only after hikes on foot for several days or a week out of the administrative fort. Considering all these handicaps, we can understand why African agents were poorly supervised by the Germans and why the Kaguru themselves were often able to avoid many German policies. The political changes in the lives of Kaguru at this time sprang more from the pressures exerted by their own ambitious leaders, who sought to use their roles to seek favor from the Germans so as to advance local influence and wealth.

## Recent Colonial Rule

The British defeated the Germans and took over most of German East Africa after World War I, instituting important changes in the formal political structure of the entire colony, including Kaguruland. These were formulated on what was then called the policy of Indirect Rule, a plan modeled after colonial experiences in India and northern Nigeria, where the British had encountered vast populations and indigenous, highly developed centralized political states. Many now consider such policies to have been, at best, naïve and inept and, at worst, used cynically to divide, retard, and exploit a subject people. In Kaguruland they created a peculiar and paradoxical political system.[1]

Cameron, the Governor most responsible for these political innovations, described his policies thus:[2]

> . . . if we preserve the tribal authority, gradually purging native law and custom of all that offends against justice and morality, building up a system for the administration of the affairs of the tribe by its hereditary rulers, with their ad-

---

[1] The situation was not as peculiar as it first appears. It occurs in all highly heterogeneous societies in which power is lodged in only a few geographically segregated subgroups, for example, urban governments with large ethnic ghettos, state governments with economic and population imbalance between urban and rural areas, and national governments of nations with important regional differences.

[2] Ironically, Cameron's speech was apparently found radical in the 1920s, whereas it seems reactionary today. For details on his policies see Cameron 1939:31–36, 75–82, 171–177, 194–197, 282–285.

visors according to native custom, we immediately give the natives a share in the government of the country, and that, moreover, on lines which they themselves understand and can appreciate. The position given to the chiefs in this way will be jealously guarded by them and their people, especially against the assaults which may in the course of time be made against it by Europeanized natives seeking to obtain political control of the country and to govern it entirely on European lines. We are not only giving the natives a share in the administration of the country but we are at the same time building up a bulwark against political agitators. At the same time a discipline and authority by the Chief which the people will understand will be preserved and we shall avert the social chaos which would ensue if every native could do exactly as he pleased so long as he did not come into conflict with the law. The Chiefs are much better equipped to punish their tribesmen than we are under a system of British laws and we have given them their own Courts for that purpose. To break down the only form of discipline and authority that the natives know and then to cry out that they are rapidly becoming more and more ill-disciplined is merely to admit failure. and to admit it without realizing the causes that underlies [sic] that failure. There is no doubt at all in my mind that the economic progress of the country must be set back if a condition of affairs arises in which the influence that we bring to bear through the natural rulers of the people disappears and the native can do as he pleases. [Great Britain 1927:7–9.]

These policies were clearly inconsistent, for it was claimed at one and the same time that Indirect Rule would gradually train colonial peoples to rule themselves but that it would also establish or strengthen local traditional groups which would resist attempts toward modern political movements such as nationalism and anticolonial self-determinism. In the final period of British rule in Kaguruland there was deep animosity between local administrators of Indirect Rule and the young militants who later became the new leaders of an independent African nation.

The British initiated this policy in Kaguruland in the 1920s under the governorship of Cameron, a former civil servant in Nigeria. However, these policies were hardly applied in the same manner throughout the colony. Although it was said that the new policies would make use of tribal groups as bases for government, some government districts were formed otherwise. The Kaguru as a group were ignored in drawing boundaries. Kaguruland was divided between two different provinces: two-thirds, the eastern portion, where I did fieldwork, was allocated to what the British called the Eastern Province, and the remainder, to the west, to the Central Province. This division has continued since African independence. It created difficulties for Kaguru living nearby one another but in different provinces. For example, these Kaguru might wish to take one another to court or try to draft common policies on livestock control or health, but they are forced to work through two different provincial administrations with all the red tape and higher policy decisions invariably involved in a government bureaucracy.

The procedures by which Indirect Rule was set up in Kaguruland differed in the two provinces; I describe how this was done in the Eastern Province, where I worked. The province was divided into several districts, each headed by a European district commissioner assisted by two or three assistant district commissioners. There were also a number of specialists such as an agricultural officer and a medical officer, who directed services in the district. The commissioners were in charge of administration and controlled and articulated the activities of the other European officials, but were in turn directly responsible to their respective officers at the provincial level. At times there were conflicts and differences between policies instituted in different services. In the eyes of Kaguru, the European colonial service presented a homogeneous front, but in reality the colonial administration was a complex hierarchy with tensions caused by the competition of its various administrators, seeking to advance their careers through the records of their achievements and their standing as contrasted with competing officers and other departments. Many inconsistencies and reversals in policies which mystified Kaguru were due to the internal struggles for power and prestige by ruling Europeans. The Europeans themselves consciously strove to present a solid front to those they governed. A mere handful of Europeans attempted to govern an area the size of a small American state with over a quarter of a million people speaking five or six languages. The Europeans and most of the Africans spoke the lingua franca of East Africa, Swahili, though it was not a language much spoken by locals themselves except in the towns and market centers, where there was a mixture of tribal groups. In the rural areas the traditional languages persisted.

Thus the British administrators faced many difficulties: They were few in number while the area was large in population and size; the range of tasks assigned was huge, yet they were relatively ignorant of local problems and traditions; they spoke Swahili but not the local African languages; their service itself was divided into competing and semiautonomous administrative units; and transport within the area, especially during the rainy season, was difficult. Furthermore, local policy prevented an administrator from gaining deep familiarity with his district, for men were sent home on leave after three years of service and were not usually allowed to remain in a particular district more than two consecutive tours, supposedly because circulation would give them the broader perspective necessary for advancement to higher positions later on.

## The Kaguru Native Authority

The formal administrative unit by which Kaguru were to govern themselves was called the Kaguru Native Authority. This was a miniature replica of the colonial administration with a hierarchy of African officials responsible to the European administrative officers and Africans employed in the specialized services. The Kaguru Native Authority was officially said to be semiautonomous, but it was recognized by everyone that, in fact, all important decisions rested with European supervisors. Some British administrators intended to dominate in this way, but in part this situation was simply due to the fact that most of the Kaguru in such posts were so poorly educated that they were unable to make administrative decisions responsibly. There were, of course, educated Kaguru, but the salaries paid to Kaguru Native Authority officials were too small to attract competent men. The salary of the average headman was less than half that of a domestic servant in a European household, while even the salary of the paramount chief was far less than that of the lower qualified African elementary teachers.

Officially, the Kaguru Native Authority could issue rulings and was responsible for how part of the taxes collected in the area were used; in practice these decisions were made by the British. Kaguru were said to be allowed to elect their own headmen and chiefs though these had to be approved by the British and could be removed by them without grounds or justification.

The British claimed that since Kaguru put forward their own traditional leaders to be officials in the Native Authority, these would have the cooperation of their people. But the needs of the British were opposed to tradition. The British required a hierarchical administration with a paramount chief at the top, four sub-chiefs under him, and headmen below, whereas in the past, at least before the Arabs interfered with Kaguru affairs, leaders were not ranked but equal. Although the British recognized clan membership as the criterion for election of such officials, that is, one for each separate clan-owned area, they were not prepared to accept over one-hundred such officials. Instead, they created fifty-four head-manships, putting unrecognized clan areas under those that were. In creating four subchiefdoms, they simply chose four sites which were geographically convenient for building administrative centers, and the clan owning such a site provided the subchief. Many Kaguru bitterly remarked how some clans were indeed lucky with colonialism. The main prop to this system was the Native Authority court, where persons could bring disputes for settlement and where the government prosecuted wrongdoers. These courts could fine, imprison, or dispense corporal punishment (flogging), but large fines (over 1,000 shillings, or $140), long imprisonment (over one year), and capital punishment could only be dispensed by European magistrates. These courts enforced judgments on civil divorce, repayments of debts, and other disputes. Each subchief and the paramount chief had a court and had from six to nineteen headmen under him. Judgments by the subchiefs could be appealed to the paramount chief's court. The largest court area was controlled directly by the paramount chief and contained over 17,000 people, while the smallest, a remote mountain subchiefdom, had only 5000 people. Some of the headmen looked after areas which were inhabited by over 4000 people and were 80 square miles in size, while some in the mountain areas had only 200 or 300 subjects and an area of only about 8 square miles.

The offices created through the Native Authority were sources of considerable power, but they created difficulties for those who assumed them. These officials stood between an alien colonial administration and their own people and were able to use this pivotal position to their own advantages. It was assumed by his people that a headman could better explain and judge their problems to the Europeans than they themselves could; he could work out matters as benefited the local situation and then present some version of this to the outsiders which would lead them not to interfere. Conversely, the Europeans, with their ignorance about the details of local affairs, depended on headmen for on-the-spot implementation of colonial policies. It has been said that colonial rule, as formulated officially on paper, was unrealistic, unworkable and unenforceable; but a semblance of the official model of rule could be preserved because of the gap in communication between the various levels of government. Local Kaguru leaders reported only what seemed to their advantage or, at the most, only those additional bits of unpleasant information their superiors seemed likely to learn anyway. In conveying colonial

*A Kaguru Native Authority employee in uniform.*

policies to their people these same Kaguru officials often modified them to their own advantage. Manipulation occurred at the higher levels of European administration as well. Different departments withheld and doctored reports in order to increase their budgets and prestige within the civil service, while junior administrators groomed reports in order to present a good image to their superiors to secure advancement. At all levels there was great discrepancy between official written reports and the realities of the situation.[3]

Tax collection provides a good illustration of these processes. Every year the government collected taxes from the local Kaguru population. These provided the major source of income for the government. The staff at local courts collected funds, and their clerks issued lists of living taxpayers which were checked against census figures to estimate the number of new payers each year due to birth and

[3] A similar situation exists in many bureaucratic organizations, especially those such as government, highly subsidized business, and the military, where real economic profit and efficiency are not always criteria for survival.

migration. Local officials were expected to remit taxes corresponding to the amount estimated. Inevitably, these figures were somewhat inaccurate. From this arrangement sprang the power of local officials, for every local official was allowed to waive taxation in some cases and could also use discretion in deciding when young men were eligible to be put on the tax rolls. Now headmen control such information and pass this on to their subchief or chief at the court center. A headman must make most people pay taxes, but he can blame this necessary evil on the government; furthermore, he can favor those who have helped him, bribed him, or are related to him and can punish his enemies by selectively enforcing or overlooking the rules. Within this marginal area of cases which the headman may enforce, modify, or ignore lies a field in which he can reward or punish those subjects who are of most concern to him in keeping order and advancing his own influence. It does not require many cases for a headman to demonstrate his power, if not directly, then by example of what may happen to others in the future seeking his support. How much a headman can manipulate is related to the number of people he governs, but it is also dependent upon the chief's evaluation of his tax returns which are submitted to the British.

The same pattern may be found in other activities where the discretionary powers of headmen are important, such as drafting labor for government work, settlement of disputes outside of court, testimony for or against one by a headman in court cases, reporting of offenses, for example, assault, improper agricultural practices, or wife beating. Sometimes headmen will overlook such offenses if news does not leak out from his area, but whether he does or not depends greatly upon his attitude toward those involved.

The headman represents the lowest level of government official whose proper commands should be followed by Kaguru. However, he himself cannot legally judge disputes, exact fines, or give punishment. Headmen often delegate unofficial assistants considerable power even though such men are not recognized by the government and the creation of unofficial deputies is officially illegal. Headmen also often hear cases and exact fines. Kaguru may first try to have a headman hear a case rather than take it to court, for one must pay a fee to go to court and then entrust judgment to an official who may not be sympathetic or responsive to one's own needs. In some cases, such as divorce, adultery, or assault between kin, those involved may want to avoid the public exposure at court if at all possible. It often happens that they will bring a case to a headman for settlement and illegally pay him a fee for his time and trouble. This is only possible where the disputants are kin or neighbors subject to common moral pressures to work out their differences.

Every Kaguru neighborhood is made up of many homesteads or hamlets (kaya). A few men, because of their kin affiliations, age, and experience, are recognized as leaders or spokesmen by many of the inhabitants of a settlement or neighborhood. A headman often states publicly that such men are his assistants. He will make a point of drinking with them, and asking them to accompany him to court when cases concerning their neighbors are heard to provide them the prestige of association with his office. These men are said to have his ear and gain influence with their own subordinates. In return they provide the headman with information and advice on local affairs. In practice each headman has a number of subordinates who represent the leadership of the most important factions within his area. There are no formal rules to such a relationship; it is simply a reciprocal tie of mutual advantage to be broken by either.

A headman has few formal punishments which he can legally apply without consulting his chief or subchief; his own power is kept in check since he requires a minimum of popular support by these leaders if he is to secure the information and cooperation for fulfilling his obligations to his superiors. An unpopular headman can be sabotaged effectively by his people. He is dependent upon "delivering the goods" to at least some of his people if he wants the bribes, favors, and gifts they give him in return for smoothing their way in difficulties with the government. A headman is selected by the owner clan. Usually he is a member of that clan; less often he is the son of such a man. He is chosen because he can be controlled by his elder kinsmen since they remain the sources of much of his power; after all, they are usually the largest single clan group in the area, and they are already bound to him in terms of various marriage payments and debts and through the sentiments of kinship. Sometimes a weak person, perhaps a mere son of a clan man, may be elected as a "front" behind whom an elder who dislikes publicity and confronting Europeans may then actually direct affairs. In any disputes a headman is said nearly always to favor his kin if at all possible.

## Kaguru Court Cases

I now consider ten cases brought to Kaguru courts. Each illustrates one or more facets in the wide range of powers by which Kaguru officials manipulate their people. I present each case and then comment upon it.

### Case A

Masige brought Chisengo to court; Chisengo had married Masige's sister but was said not to have paid all of the bridewealth agreed upon. In anger, Masige has harassed and threatened Chisengo. In revenge Chisengo had burned down Masige's mother's house in Masige's village. The subchief of X ruled against Chisengo and fined him heavily. Chisengo appealed the case to the paramount chief's court, which reversed the decision and let Chisengo off. Shortly thereafter, Chisengo brought a case to the court of the subchief of X. He accused Masige of assault with a deadly weapon. Furious after the house-burning incident, Masige had attacked Chisengo. Masige tried to justify himself by saying that Chisengo was sleeping with his sister without having paid proper bridewealth and that the couple had a daughter for whom no payments had been made. The subchief of X fined Masige very lightly and then advised Masige publicly to register a case against Chisengo. The subchief said, "Adultery and taking a child which is not yours are serious crimes. You make a case against Chisengo and he will be punished more heavily than you have been."

The conduct of the two courtheads, the subchief of X and the paramount chief, makes sense only if one knows more about local Kaguru politics. The two chiefs had openly quarreled and insulted one another. The paramount chief had

*Kaguru attending a political meeting led by a subchief.*

supported the European use of forced labor even though its legality was highly questionable. He had gained wealth from this but was disliked by many Kaguru. The subchief of X refused to support forced labor and sought to use his own opposition to foster his political ambitions, which were directed toward forming several parapolitical associations outside the formal Native Authority. These associations resembled vigilante groups such as those found in the Old American West.[4] It was said by Kaguru that the enmity between the chiefs probably led the one chief to reverse the other's judgment. Chisengo had long been critical of the subchief of X. He sought to use the enmity between that subchief and the paramount chief to his own advantage. However, many Kaguru felt that this was unwise. Thus, even when Chisengo had a just case, he received only minimal satisfaction and the subchief openly aided his enemy, Masige. Now it is true that Chisengo could continue to appeal his cases to the paramount chief, but this would cost much time and trouble and be a gamble. The subchief seemed likely to continue to stir up difficulties for Chisengo, who, with his bad temper and domestic troubles, was prone to many disputes. Kaguru say that it is foolish to offend a headman or subchief even when you are in the right and, for the moment, might win, for the official can always wait for other occasions when you are in the wrong and will need his help.

It may be asked how a courtholder would be allowed to make such partisan comments (by European standards) in a colonial court. For one thing,

---

[4] I discuss these elsewhere (Beidelman 1961b).

the European staff was too small for them to monitor such cases. They had to rely upon written summaries of the cases which were turned in by the court, and they also relied upon the hope that really outrageous conduct would be appealed to them. Court records were compiled by local officials so as to omit any incriminating or embarrassing material. Sometimes cases were not recorded at all. Then courtholders and clerks who kept the records divided the unrecorded fines and fees between themselves. In any case, the words "outrageous" or "corrupt" depended upon the assumption of British values regarding the legitimacy and purpose of the courts; to Kaguru such terms had no such connotations.

Few disgruntled Kaguru would report court abuses to Europeans. It was a dangerous thing to annoy local officials with whom one had to continue to live. Kaguru often found that unless gross infringement of European powers (such as using force without European approval) were concerned, European administrators usually simply referred a case back to the local courts, arguing that they did not want to undermine the respect and authority of local officials. Such appeals would have only further antagonized local leaders and not advanced one's own case at all. Furthermore, the British were aware of a fundamental contradiction between their avowed policies and the way the native authorities had actually been set up. Many spoke of the desirability of courts being neutral in the sense that the interests of the court judges should be separate from the administrators' and legislators' whose acts they judged. The same local Kaguru officials made laws, enacted them, and then judged such acts in courts. However, local officials were denied the direct use of force to control their subjects, the administration of harsh penalties and the use of police being monopolized by the British. One of the few sanctions still open to local officials lay in the form of the court verdicts themselves. Local officials could not allow diminution of one of their few remaining means of securing respect and conformity.

## Case B

Headman Amosi was said to have tried to intimidate Chiduo into moving. Chiduo brought Amosi to court and accused him of trying to make Chiduo's life unbearable so that he would abandon his home and fields and live elsewhere. Amosi announced that Chiduo was banished from his (Amosi's) land, a ban which Chiduo rightly contended was today illegal. Amosi brought seven witnesses to support his defenses, each stating that Chiduo was an undesirable person. These witnesses gave confused and garbled testimony. One of the witnesses was Amosi's deputy, who stated that Amosi and Chiduo had frequently quarreled and that this proved that Chiduo was a troublesome person. Another stated that Chiduo was undesirable because he was always getting angry with people when his fields had been trampled by livestock. Another testified that Chiduo sometimes quarreled and became violent when drunk. The court listened patiently and politely to all of this, even though, to an outsider, it seemed grossly unreasonable, for all these reported vices of Chiduo were traits common to many Kaguru and could simply be said to indicate that Chiduo was the kind of man who stood up for his rights and could not easily be intimidated. The court concluded that Chiduo did not have any legal case against Amosi. However, it avoided making any pronouncement upon the issue of the legality of Headman Amosi's attempt to banish Chiduo, an act which indeed had no legal basis. Chiduo was told that since he had no proper case, he would lose the fees paid for making the case and that he would have to pay the expenses of the seven witnesses which the accused had brought to court for his defense. These costs amounted to 24 shillings. By Kaguru standards this was tantamount to a fine against Chiduo for having made a case in court against a headman popular with the court. One cannot help suspecting collusion between the court and Headman Amosi in the allowance of such an unusually large number of witnesses whose expenses were paid by the plaintiff. The case was not recorded in the court records.

## Case C

Dansoni is a member of the paramount chief's matrilineage. One day, according to Dansoni, he saw Chibaibai leaving his (Dansoni's) house. Chibaibai is a close, joking relative (father's sister's son) to Headman Yubi, a headman under the paramount chief. Both Headman Yubi and Chibaibai are notorious philanderers, and one of the usual people with whom one can get help in sexual affairs is one's cross-cousin. Dansoni strongly criticized both Headman Yubi and Chibaibai, who serves as the headman's deputy. He told Chibaibai that he would not tolerate either Chibaibai or Yubi near his house. Chibaibai reported this to Headman Yubi, who came to Dansoni and ordered him to leave his area. Dansoni refused and reported the affair to the paramount chief, who summoned Headman Yubi. The paramount chief threatened to dismiss Headman Yubi if he did not pay adultery fines for himself and Chibaibai. He is alleged to have told Yubi, "If a headman can tell his subject to leave his land, then a chief can tell his headman to leave his land as well?" I know of no case in which a paramount chief has made good such a threat, but then this does not seem to have been the real gist of the chief's words. He seems to have been telling Yubi that he thought Yubi had tried to intimidate Dansoni by illegal means and that this could be reported to the British—for no one can banish a person from his area (except the British, who did so on occasion). Furthermore, the paramount chief could complicate Headman Yubi's affairs in court cases and government affairs so that Yubi could hardly afford to exacerbate the chief's ill will. Yubi paid a fine of one goat and 80 shillings, which was divided between the chief and his kinsman, Dansoni. Local Kaguru now feel that Yubi has lost considerable prestige and Dansoni has felt safe in publicly insulting Yubi. It is likely that Yubi was drunk when he threatened Dansoni, otherwise he might not have acted so recklessly in a way which cost him wealth and influence. A headman may legally be dismissed by a subchief or the paramount chief, but this is unlikely. In any case, the support of a courthead is very important to a headman's power, and any withdrawal of such authority, even in the case of a recalcitrant man such as Headman Yubi, would often bring him to heel. Headmen and chiefs need not be friends, but they need one another to bolster their mutual authority. With the support of a chief's court, a headman is able to weather the anger of a larger group of his own subjects; without it, even his ordinary subjects may give him difficulty. Correspondingly, a chief needs his headmen to provide him with information and the taxes and labor the British require.

The bitter enmity between the paramount chief and Headman Yubi was due to events many years before his chiefly appointment. Then the paramount chief was poor and sick and not considered likely to hold his present position. He lived in Headman Yubi's area and asked him to obtain a tax exemption, pleading that he was unable to pay due to ill health. Yubi is said to have requested a calabash of beer and some cash before he would submit the elder's name to the list for exemption. The future chief was fined as a tax defaulter and spent a few days in jail until his kinsmen paid his tax. Kaguru say this illustrates the fact that one should be very careful about offending others, for one never knows who may hold power one day.

Case D

Some members of the dominant clan of Y resented their headman, Tutiyo. One faction supported Headman Tutiyo, while the other demanded his replacement by their favorite. Each faction insisted that its rivals were not of the dominant clan but were only freed slaves who had usurped clan rights. The issue had come to a head over the slaying of a cow to celebrate the opening of a new mission school in the Y area. Tutiyo had provided a cow and then requested contributions from the other members of his clan to recompense him for this. His supporters contributed, but the other faction refused. The dissidents sought the support of the local court subchief, but he supported Headman Tutiyo since he and Tutiyo had cooperated together in court cases for years. This dispute was then brought to the court of the subchief and decided in favor of Headman Tutiyo. The other faction contested this decision and appealed to the paramount chief. Both Headman Tutiyo and the subchief of X had quarreled with the chief over the issue of forced labor. The paramount chief was invited to Y and was entertained by the dissident faction, which, according to many Kaguru, may have given him many gifts. The subchief's verdict was reversed by the paramount chief when the case was appealed to him. Headman Tutiyo and the subchief of X then appealed the case to the district administration, which supported Tutiyo, saying that it disliked frequent changes in the administration and the use of Native Authority posts as "footballs" in clan politics. Tutiyo himself had an excellent record as headman. The case was appealed to the provincial administration, which supported the district administration.

Case E

The following statement is part of a court's verdict on an assault case:

> The accused has admitted his offense of having beaten his mother while he was drunk. The court levies a fine of 20 shillings and a payment of 10 shillings compensation to the mother. If the accused does not pay this amount of 30 shilling because he has no goods, he will be locked up in jail for one month hard labor. When he returns, he must pay 10 shillings compensation.

Such procedure is not usually resorted to unless the court is already fairly sure that the accused has kinsmen who will make such a payment once he has been jailed. Otherwise, a smaller payment may be asked by the court, which has little desire to confine a prisoner. Confinement is inconvenient in a Kaguru jail, for the local staff must tend the prisoner or arrange for his shipment to the district capital. Kaguru see justice primarily in terms of awarding indemnity to a person who has been wronged and has suffered, not merely as punishment of a criminal. The fines collected by the court are justified because they pay officials' salaries, construct government buildings, and provide other services. Kaguru ask why a murderer should be sent to jail since this does little good for the kin of the victim who suffer by the death. Kaguru would say that more good would be achieved were murderers made to pay the victim's kin. They ask what good is gained by these kin if the man is jailed and then works for the government: "Has the government or the bereaved relatives suffered more from the death? Why doesn't it go to the ones who really suffered?" In the past the kinsmen of the murderer would have had to pay bloodwealth to the victim's kin. If no wealth were readily available, they might even have sold the murderer into slavery or pawnage to secure such wealth.

## Case F

A Gogo was accused by the headman of K of seducing the headman's wife.[5] The headman's children reported this to their father. The Gogo had been taken in during a serious famine in Gogoland. He had worked for the headman and accumulated a small amount of wealth, which was confiscated by the headman in compensation for the adultery: three goats, 61 shillings, two gardens of maize, and a box of cloth. This was an extreme departure from the customary punishment for adultery in which a Kaguru would be fined 10 shillings and pay 60 shillings compensation to the offended person. The Gogo had appealed the case to the district commissioner at Kilosa, who refused to hear the case, referring it back to the local court. The Gogo admitted his adultery and had at first accepted the contested judgment, apparently only later fully grasping its departure from the Kaguru norms. No one supported the Gogo, who was a tribal alien in Kaguruland. Kaguru felt that the Gogo deserved a very heavy fine because he had betrayed the man who had befriended him. No such extra considerations ever seemed to figure in the many purely Kaguru adultery cases which I heard during my three year stay in the area. Kaguru apply a double standard in punishing themselves and tribal outsiders in their courts. As a rule, tribal outsiders are judged more harshly. The justification often given is that such people are wealthier and therefore should pay more in order to feel truly punished so that they will not commit such crimes again. Others argue that since the offenders are outsiders, they are more difficult to control and require harsher sanctions to keep them in check.

## Case G

An old Kamba-Gogo woman complained that her headman had sent his messengers to beat her.[6] She and other women had been summoned to draw water for the district commissioner and his staff, who were staying for several days at

---

[5] I record this case elsewhere (Beidelman 1968:28–29).
[6] I discuss this case in a previous paper (Beidelman 1968:31).

the Y resthouse. She drew one jar of water and so did the other women. The others, who were Kaguru, were then allowed to leave, but when she tried to go, she was told that she should continue drawing water. She claimed that this was unfair and tried to leave. She said she was being discriminated against because she was a tribal outsider. The court admitted that the headman's deputies had usurped one of the court's basic rights by punishing offenders. In any case, it was illegal for even a court to order a woman to be beaten. The court fined these persons the sum of 5 shillings, an extremely small fine, even by Kaguru stand- ards. Before the payment was made the court told the old woman that she herself would be accused by the messengers whom she had accused, saying that she had disobeyed her headman's orders, given through the messengers, and that this offense would involve a heavy fine. The subchief added that if the old woman would withdraw her case, the court would forget about the entire matter and make no countercharge against her. The old woman left. The affair was not entered in the court records. The old woman's charges were very serious and might well have got the headman in serious trouble were such information passed on the European officials at the district capital. The court seemed to have counted on the ignorance of the old woman, who was easily intimidated by the court.

A British official's visit well illustrates how local Kaguru officials can apply sanctions to their subjects. In the eyes of Kaguru the tour of inspection of a new district commissioner required that he be provided with various services and entertainment in order to show that he was welcome. (When I jokingly suggested to British officials that their "warm welcomes" were not always the spontaneous and cordial affairs they claimed, I was coolly told that I had little knowledge of local affairs.) Water and food had to be brought for the visitor and his entourage, and local people were told that they should turn out to dance for their guest. Some were told to provide beer for the dancers. A few were directed to bring goods or to dance and were punished when they refused; others were not even asked to get involved. The local Kaguru official in charge of these affairs was thus able to punish those of his subjects of whom he disapproved by singling them out for duties of hospitality.

## Case H

Hogla is a female head of a small settlement. She accused a man in her settlement of securing a brewing license without informing her, an action which Hogla claimed scorned her authority as head of a settlement. Hogla made beer that day but was not allowed to sell this in her own settlement; instead, she had to carry this to a distant beer club with a licensed owner. She complained that had she known someone near at hand held a license, she could have sold beer there without going so far. Hogla's implicit argument was that it was unfair to expect her to sell beer at a distant settlement where she had no influence; had she been allowed to sell beer in her own settlement, she would have been spared much expense, for a subordinate would surely not have asked her to pay him. The court rejected Hogla's argument and took the court fee which she had paid to register the case. The court maintained that all people who brewed beer should buy licenses and that since she had purchased no license, she had no right to complain at all. This seemed rather hypocritical on the part of the court since it was commonly accepted in Kaguruland that beer licenses were very costly and that one person would buy a license and then, for a small payment, allow many others to sell at his place under the one covering license. Hogla was advised to stop complaining if she herself did not want to be prosecuted for brewing without a licence. The plaintiff suddenly found herself to be the accused, for the court judge was a close kinsman of the proprietor of the beer club where Hogla usually sold her beer.

### Case I

A man accused his sister of keeping a cow which had been part of his inheritance from their dead brother. The woman brought two of her sisters and her son as witnesses to support her defense. However, the court supported the accuser even though he had brought no one to support his claim against these witnesses. An elderly kinsman of the litigants, a man of the deceased's father's matrilineage (a traditional spokesman at funerals) strongly condemned the accuser and supported the women. He said, however, that he could see that the case was lost because of the court. I did not understand the meaning of his bitter remarks or why the court discounted the testimony of the many people supporting the accused. The chief of the court awarded the cow to the accuser and then said, "Now see my newphew since you now have wealth!" I asked others at the court what he had meant and learned that over a year before, the court chief's sister's son had loaned the accuser 100 shillings and that until now the accuser had given many excuses for not repaying his debt.

### Case J

The subchief of P ruled that a Native Authority road should be widened in the vicinity of his court. Kaguru with fields on the land in question were told to resign themselves to the loss of the crops planted but still unharvested upon the land. Some of the land was cleared, but two Kaguru, a schoolteacher and a former schoolteacher, protested and threatened to write to the British in the district headquarters. This was not necessary, for after their complaints, their fields were left untouched by the road builders.

## Conclusions

The preceding cases indicate the basic features of Kaguru political affairs and how the organization of local government supported the powers of certain individuals.[7] One of the ironies of local government during the colonial period is that it intensified tribalism. Kaguru were able to use their monopoly of local government to intimidate tribal minorities in their midst. The creation of a

---

[7] Elsewhere I expand on many of these points (Beidelman 1967b, 1968, and see Further Readings, under *The Kaguru*, Beidelman 1961c).

Native Authority along tribal lines meant that many sources of power and profit, such as local government jobs and education in Native Authority schools, fostered tribal consciousness. The policy of governing "on the cheap" also meant that the underpaid jobs of the Native Authority failed to attract well-educated and vigorous younger Kaguru, who, if not employed by the mission, went into work outside the area and became interested in the politics of national independence. As a result, local Kaguru officials were conservative in outlook and aware that they continued to exist only so long as the British supported an artificial power structure, which worked only so long as these foreigners themselves provided the know-how and funds to supplement the inherent inefficiencies and ineptitudes of such ill-trained local personnel. This was convenient to local British officials, who tended to use the local Native Authority government as a rubber stamp for their own political decisions.

# 7

# The Person Through Time

## Introduction

**M**ANY YEARS AGO in his classic study *Les Rites de Passage* Arnold van Gennep remarked upon the similarities in form and content of various ceremonies or rituals by which people attempt to move persons from one social category to another. Undoubtedly, the most important of these passages relate to the situations of birth, initiation into adulthood, marriage, and death. By considering these in detail we can see what symbolic values are attached to and define various social roles or categories. For example, by seeing what symbols are evoked when initiating a boy into manhood, we may observe by what values a people define manhood and masculinity. Kaguru are especially concerned with the rituals associated with birth, initiation, marriage, and death, and they sometimes speak of the comparable aspects of these four situations.

As van Gennep himself pointed out, a set of rituals used in changing from one social status to another is no simple, abrupt affair. Instead, one journeys from one social status to another through a series of way stations. The signs for these stations are expressed through various symbols of substance, space, and time. These symbols refer to subtle changes in one's character and to those qualities by which one defines oneself and is defined by others. These attributes must be changed if one is to take on a new status and shed an old one. These qualities are expressed through various other symbols of sexuality, humanity, occupation, and social ties. In the preceding chapter on Kaguru cosmology some of the broader aspects of this symbolic language were suggested: the contrast between the lands of the dead and the living, between the wild world of the bush and the more orderly world of the settlement and men; and the sensual qualities associated with men and women, and the complex use of oral, tactile, and manual symbols to express moral values and changes. Kaguru values and beliefs are related to social organization and social relations, to the ways people respond to one another on the occasions of primary social events and crises. Some of the rituals associated with Kaguru birth, initiation, marriage, and death will be described here, proceeding from birth to death.

If the reader has understood the preceding chapters on social organization and especially the chapter on cosmology, he should be able to use much of the following material to construct fairly complex analyses of Kaguru symbolism, showing how this relates to social values and social interaction. I provide some discussion here and considerably more in other publications cited in the readings and references at the back of this study, but I intend the following pages as material to encourage independent analysis by the reader himself.

## Birth

Kaguru see birth as a precarious passage from the sphere of the land of the ghosts to that of the living. The creation of a human being is seen as a long and complex process which must be carefully regulated in order to guarantee the security and stability of the newly formed person and also to protect those associated with the new child, for pregnancy and birth also place the infant's parents and other close kin in a state where they are especially vulnerable to forces which might threaten their proper, ordered relations with one another. Menstruation is associated with female fertility, and the temporary cessation of menstruation is associated with pregnancy. Some Kaguru say that during the early months of a pregnancy a husband should "feed" the womb by having frequent intercourse with his wife. The couple should refrain from intercourse during the final weeks lest the child is damaged. Sometimes a woman has difficulty conceiving or retaining a pregnancy; she may then persuade her husband to consult a diviner to determine the cause. The husband will pay for the medicines the diviner prescribes. These disruptive forces are sometimes associated with the ghosts of ancestors who do not want to give up the unborn to the living. Often one sees a Kaguru woman with unusually long hair or with an infant wearing an odd topknot. One then knows that such a person is under a diviner's care and is observing various prohibitions, of which hair grooming is one, until the child is firmly entrenched in the land of the living.

The wife should observe any food prohibitions observed by her husband since she is carrying his child. She should avoid travel, but not from fear of undue exertion on her part, for she is encouraged to work and even to cultivate her fields; she avoids travel to escape the sphere of strangers who may be hostile to her. She should refrain from honey and sugarcane, for they would make her pelvis narrow and hard and cause a difficult delivery; she should not eat eggs lest her child be born lacking head hair. Her husband should be faithful to her, and though he may sleep with his other wives, any adulterous connection is said to endanger the pregnancy. An unfaithful wife is said to have difficulty in childbirth. Kaguru sometimes say that a woman will confess her lovers during labor in order to ease her delivery, and some cynical men say that this is the real reason why women do not let men nearby when they deliver. Others say it is because the blood and afterbirth are too polluting.

Usually, a regular midwife delivers the child though some say that a woman's first child should, if possible, be delivered by her own mother. When the child is born, the women present begin to ullulate, once if it is a boy, in sets of two runs of trills if it is a girl. Neighbors and kin are expected to visit the homestead, bringing small token gifts of coins or food. The midwife is given a small payment in cash or tobacco and provides various medicines to guarantee that the child develops properly, for the child is not yet considered safely out of the land of the ghosts. The next few years of its life are a slow process of establishing a foothold in the world of the living. This is not completed until the child is initiated into adulthood. Until then, it cannot become a ghost if it dies, for to die fully one must be fully alive, and it has never become fully free from the ghostly realm and is not yet a morally responsible person.

For the first three or four days after birth the mother and infant may not leave the house and are tended by the midwife and the mother's kin, especially the women of her own matrilineage. The umbilical cord has been cut and tied, but the child and mother should not emerge until this has dried up and dropped free from the child and is secretly buried. This marks the next sign of the child's slow passage out of the land of the ghosts. However, the navel remains a part of the body which provides a vulnerable entry into the inner nature of a person; thus, even in lovemaking people would not like to touch such areas. Another vulnerable body area is the soft area atop an infant's head. It is said that the child breathes through this. Kaguru use many medicines to protect these parts of infants, especially against sorcery and witchcraft. When the child and mother first emerge from the house, there is a ceremony called Growing (*kukula*) which marks the falling away of the umbilical cord. The father provides food and beer and his sister comes with medicine to prevent the child from being attacked by birds of prey.

Somewhat later there is another ritual, Shaving (*kugeta*), which is held only for a couple's first two children. Now a child is given its first name. The firstborn child is shaved by its maternal kin, who in return are given a small gift by the child's father. The secondborn child is shaved by its paternal kin. Later the father's sister and his mother return and pound flour, which they present to the child and which they then cook and eat. All of these acts are said to protect the child in its problematical first confrontations outside its mother's womb, where it must now deal with both hostile nature and various difficult humans. If the child cries often or is repeatedly ill, it may be given additional names of deceased kin who have been divined as causing its illness. A small child may thus have a large number of names, although to deflect the attention and jealousy of others it may also simply be referred to as "Ugly One" or "Unwanted One" or some other misleadingly negative term.

If a child were born improperly, as a twin or in a breech delivery, it would have been strangled immediately since it was regarded as an abnormal creature endangering its kin. However, physical signs of dangerous and unusual power may not appear until the child cuts its first teeth, perhaps the most definitive sign that it is truly likely to remain among the living as a normal and unproblematical member of society. The infant wears white beads to "cool" it, to keep it normal and therefore unlikely to cut its upper teeth first. It should be killed if it does so. Once its teeth have appeared normally, parents express considerable pleasure and relief.

A Kaguru proverb says, "Birth is a device for eating!" meaning that birth leads to marriage, that human fertility is a source of advantage and profit since it provides new persons to work, connect one to new people through marriage, help one in old age, and carry on one's name and memory after death. Yet birth is filled with dangers and problems, the most serious being delivery itself, especially in the past, when no facilities were available for difficult birth. Kaguru are right to speak of childbirth as warfare (*ng'hondo*) for like warfare, birth brings booty in the form of children and prestige, but it can bring death and misfortune as well for all concerned.

Small children are sometimes nursed for a year or more; it is thought that pregnancy causes a woman's milk to dry up. Many Kaguru recommend that a woman should avoid full intercourse so long as they are nursing. Some say that a nursing mother who gets pregnant has no shame or concern for her previous child.

When little girls begin to toddle, they are given fiber aprons; but little boys may go about naked until they are quite old. When children can assume small tasks and wander about nearby alone with safety, they are encouraged to eat with their own sex, for sexes should eat separately on all occasions.

## Initiation

Kaguru see initiation as a process which converts irresponsible, immature minors into morally responsible adults. A person cannot exert jural controls over other or properly propitiate ghosts until he or she has gone through initiation. It is a way of "cooking" raw children into "palatable" adults which may be comfortably digested by society. It entails both physical operations and moral instruction regarding the way initiates will be expected to conduct themselves in the future. As in brainwashing in political groups and hazing by fraternal organizations, the physical distress and irregularities of these rites may make the individual more disposed toward accepting and internalizing new values and modes of conduct; physical violence to the person is a common part of the indoctrination of new members both to the military and to prisons. Most Kaguru insist that initiation was, indeed, the most important and impressive experience in their lives, and most conduct themselves in a different tone and style after they have undergone such rituals.

Kaguru sometimes call initiation a kind of marriage since it opens the way to permitted sexual activity and eventual marriage. While individual adultery cases are usually criticized by those directly involved and who thereby may suffer from such acts, clandestine sexual activities are accepted by most Kaguru as natural and inevitable, provided that both the persons involved have been through initiation. Initiation is further compared to divorce since it too is an act of separation from previous ties. Initiation is also sometimes compared both to birth and to death. Like birth it opens a new world of life to a person but like birth, too, it involves danger, especially in the operations performed on boys, although I have never heard of a death from circumcision. Kaguru say that with initiation one dies as a child to be reborn as an adult, a metaphor quite similar to many expressions in English related to religious conversion. Many aspects of initiation are common to men and women, including many of the riddles and songs learned by

*Kaguru boys.*

*A Kaguru youth (right), newly circumcised, being comforted and advised by another youth; note the horn of medicine stuck into the ground near the base of the sapling.*

each as a way of being indoctrinated into proper sexual behavior. However, Kaguru see both the purposes of the two physical operations (circumcision of men and labiadectomy of women) and the particular result of the accompanying ritual as basically different.

# Boys' Initiation

In the past boys were initiated in large groups, sometimes containing as many as a hundred. This involved persons from many adjoining neighborhoods and reflected the influence of a few prominent leaders who sponsored such ceremonies. Today most initiations involve only a few boys and rarely only a single person. Local leaders will try to encourage as many boys as possible to be cut, partly in order to augment their own prestige as the organizers of large affairs and partly to involve as many elders as possible in sharing the costs of the cutter, required medicines, and the beer and food for those participating. It is thought that boys are better able to endure the operation and learn the many riddles and songs of the ceremonies if they are many and compete with one another in setting a good example. The most important persons in charge of putting a particular boy through initiation are his father and one of his mother's brothers, that is, one of the senior men of his own matrilineage. Often the ceremonies in any locale are initiated and dominated by one man who is prominent in that area because of his wealth, kin affiliations, or political connections. Along with marriage ceremonies, initiation dances and feasts are occasions by which Kaguru may conspicuously provide hospitality as a measure of their local prestige.

Circumcision takes place in the dry season. Some say this is because it is a more healthful time for these operations, while others say it is because then people have more free time than during the rains, when they are cultivating. Kaguru describe this time as good for cutting because it is dry and cool, but they may also be referring to moral attributes since the purpose of circumcision is to "cool" and "dry" a boy's sexuality, to make it unlike a woman's (hot and moist). The time and place for such ceremonies are usually decided after consulting divination. A circumcisor is chosen for his skill in cutting and his medicines, which protect his patient from both physical and supernatural dangers. Often a man may be hired from a considerable distance.

On the morning of the announced day people assemble and the chosen boys, along with their sponsors and attendants, are led into the bush, where a clearing and a lean-to have been prepared. Along with the cutter are the boys' senior male kin and some of their friends and neighbors as well as some youths only a few years older than the boys being initiated. It is said that such youths still vividly recall their own initiation and are therefore especially sympathetic and helpful to the boys. The boys are told of the danger of the cutting and that they may die. The danger is thought to be mystical as well as physical. Not only are they out in the bush, far from the ordinary routine of the village, but they are thought especially vulnerable to the witchcraft of others. Strangers, uncircumcized persons, and women are forbidden entry into the clearing.

The boys are stripped of their clothing and shaved of all their body and head hair. This devoids them of all social statuses of their past and marks them as clean and impressionable to the roles they have ahead of them. The doctor ritually cools his knives in water and uses various medicines and charms, many with prominent white (cooling) symbols in order to protect the boys and purify his instruments. White cocks are slain and their feathers used to make fans for cooling the boys' wounds. Those present sing, "People! The lion is biting the cow!" The themes of danger and the wild and powerful but destructive animals of the bush are prominent in much of the ceremony.

It is prestigious to be the first cut. The boy's elder kinsmen hold him down in a sitting position while he is cut. It is considered admirable to endure the cutting silently and without flinching, but those who cry or flinch are not condemned or taunted. It is said that in the past boys were quite old when they were circumcized. Today they are often cut when only ten or twelve years old so that few expect much bravery from them. However, it is considered somewhat shameful to be cut at a hospital or dispensary, partly because the songs and other ritual cannot then accompany the cutting, but more important because such medical facilities are usually frequented by many women. The foreskin is cut off, removing the "low, wet, dirty" feminine-like part of the boy. The bloodied objects are buried secretly by the cutter. The boys are helped to the lean-to, where they are restrained from moving by means of various contraptions of wood and cord. The elders build a fire and feed the boys, who are considered to be helpless like babies.

Each day women of the boys' villages come to the edge of the clearing and sing that they are bringing food to the boys, who are compared to hungry nestlings just out of their eggs. The men take the flour, vegetables, and other supplies brought by the women and cook and feed the boys. Ordinarily, men would never be involved in cooking tasks, which are the work of women. Whenever a man comes to visit the clearing for the first time, he sings that he is arriving limping due to his sadness and pity for the wounded boys. Each visitor should bring a small token gift of coins or beer for those present. The boys are forbidden to wash but are kept "cool" and "clean" by being covered with white ashes. Kaguru say the boys are "anointed" with ashes, just as they will later be anointed with oil when they are named and blessed as new adults. Each day they are taught many songs and riddles. Some relate to various ceremonies connected with initiation itself, such as the songs sung to greet visitors and the songs later sung when the boys leave the initiation camp to return home. Most of these songs and riddles relate to the teaching of proper sexual behavior and knowledge. They usually take the form of a short song or verse with a hidden meaning. In explaining the deeper, hidden meanings the elders inculcate many values and ideas about Kaguru society and morality. Here are four examples:

1. "The *mupululuji* tree of the river valley is good, but it is not good to cut it for building a house.

Kaguru commonly associate river valleys with women because of the fertility and also because of wetness and lowness. Kaguru say that this song really tells that one should not have sexual relations with one's sister, even though she may be a very attractive person. Much of Kaguru folklore dwells upon the ambivalent attitudes with which Kaguru view sibling incest.

*A Kaguru circumcisor escorting the mothers of newly initiated youths to the vicinity of where the youths were cut.*

2. "Child, don't go out early in the morning or you will meet a rhinoceros with its horn slashing and exposing red flesh."

Kaguru say this tells a youth (who dwells in his bachelor's house) not to enter his parents' house too early or he may witness them having sexual relations. Any hint of sexuality, even an oblique comment, is considered very shameful between parents and children. Here, the horror of such conduct is expressed through allusions to a fierce wild animal and to redness, the color of blood, fire, danger, and death. The slashing in this song and the cutting in the preceding song reflect the aggressive tone with which Kaguru endow sexual behavior.

3. "When you cut stubble in the mountains it remains cut, but there in the lowlands one cannot see whether it has been cut at all!"

This is said to show how one can readily see that a man has been initiated because circumcision is easy to notice, but that the cutting done on females is not always discernible. The deeper meaning is that men, once initiated, are truly clean and morally responsible persons, but women are thought to be perpetually contaminated by their own fertility, that is, menstruation. This physical and moral instability in women accounts for why they should never be given moral responsibility and authority. Here, mountains (high, infertile) are associated with men while lowlands (low, fertile) are associated with women. The notion of stubble being quickly overgrown conveys the ambiguous character of fertility. There also seems to be an association of vegetation with hair, the prevalence of both (the wooded bush and an unshaved, ungroomed person) signifying moral instability but also power.

4. "The thing that cuts me on the head has slipped down and cut me below!"

It is said that the knife establishes order and cleanliness through removing unclean, unsightly material. One shaves one's head at important rituals, especially at purification after a funeral; circumcision also removes impurity, and head hair is shaved off before circumcision.

When the boys have recovered, some of the men try to frighten them by going into the bush and mimicking wild animals, especially lions and leopards. The boys are told that if they reveal these initiation secrets, they will be devoured by such beasts.

As they begin to recover, the initiates are allowed to go further from camp; however, these boys must return each night to sleep in the camp. In some areas they go about from village to village singing in groups and receiving small gifts of coins. They do this covered in fibers and straw so that their faces and bodies are concealed.

While the boys are recovering, their kin are careful that their own actions do not mystically endanger the boys. They are especially careful not to quarrel, commit adultery, or otherwise misbehave. One Kaguru legend explains the origin of baboons as due to some Kaguru not paying proper attention to recovering initiates so that their transition into adulthood became confused and they were transformed into hairy, wild creatures (see references, Beidelman 1963b).

Although Kaguru often speak about the dangers of circumcision, resultant illness and death appear very rare. If someone did die, his death would not be announced publicly and he would not be mourned, for he would not have died a regular person.

When the elders see that all the youths have recovered, they send them out on some task far from the camp. In the boys' absence, the elders burn and bury everything in the camp. When the boys return, they are surprised to find nothing left of the camp and are told that the elders have swallowed everything. The boys are kept up all night, for there is no lean-to for shelter. As they huddle about the fire, a few elders slip away from the boys and out in the bush to mimic lions, while those elders who remain try to frighten the boys by making worried comments about these weird noises. At dawn the boys wash off their ashes in a stream and are "anointed" with red earth, here associated with strength and vitality. The elders say, "The children of the elephant have bathed in mud!" (The elephant is associated with both the bush and death, and the initiates are, indeed, emerging from the bush and from a dangerous situation to be reborn as full adults.)

The youths are led out of the camp by their friends and kinsmen, singing to show that they have "conquered" the bush. The boys are now considered "half-circumcised"; the process will not be considered complete until they have enjoyed a coming-out feast and dance at which much beer and food are provided.

If a youth is poor, sometimes such ceremonies are not provided, but both he and others never feel that things were done in the respectable manner. After this dance each youth is blessed and anointed with castor oil, first by his father (on his right side), then by a maternal uncle (on his left). Anointing begins at the top of the head, where the vital soft spot existed during infancy, and proceeds to the soles of the feet. Women bless the youth by licking some of the oil from his face. As they anoint him, each blesses him and gives him a new name. Every Kaguru emerges from initiation with several proper names, each associated with certain kinsmen, living and dead.

Now the youth may engage in a full sex life, court girls, and consider marriage. Within a few years he will be required to assume some jural responsibility for his own acts, and his father may, if he wishes, let him fend for himself in legal disputes. Now, too, he will require a full funeral when he dies and will then become a true ancestral ghost. He is now a full social person.

## Girls' Initiation

Kaguru call the initiation of girls into womanhood *igubi*. The usual translation of this term is "wild pig," for some of the ceremonies make use of this porcine symbol with its implications of wildness but edibility and submission to a male huntsman. For similar reasons women sometimes figure in Kaguru legends as wild, destructive, even man-eating beasts or monsters, as bad as the wild pigs which ravage Kaguru fields at night. Some Kaguru say that the term derives from *igubike*, "being covered," since most of the ceremonies take place indoors and are concealed from men. The purpose of female initiation is to control the powers of female fertility and sexuality, to keep them in check so that they may serve social ends. Unlike male initiation, that for girls does not really alter the moral and physical nature of the initiate; rather, it merely provides an opportunity to teach girls the ways to control their inherent powers so that they will produce many children and not endanger others, especially their future husbands. Despite the scarification of the girls' genitalia and the long period of seclusion, a girl remains a permanent souce of danger and difficulty; she is not really changed. The ceremonies for girls are said to cool the girl who is hot and disordered after the onset of her first menstruation; the cutting on her genitals is said to soften her, as do other ceremonies which make her better able to bear children. (Kaguru do not practice clitoridectomy.)

Usually, female initiation is undertaken at a girl's first menstruation; thus, it may occur at any time of the year and usually involves only one girl at a time. However, Kaguru try to avoid such ceremonies during the height of the rains, when free time and surplus food are scarce. Usually, a girl's matrilineal kinswomen, especially someone of her grandmother's generation, take the lead in organizing such matters. In the past female initiation was a very complex and prolonged process. A girl was sometimes required to remain indoors for many months, sometimes for over a year. She was only allowed out in the company of her elderly supervisor, and then she had to observe many inconvenient prohibi-

*Kaguru dancing at a circumcision feast.*

*Kaguru celebrating a female initiation.*

tions. This confinement is said to have made the girl fat and pale, qualities thought to enhance her desirability for marriage. Today a girl is confined only a few days or, if she has been cut, perhaps a few weeks until she has recovered. During this time she grinds maize and performs other household chores for her kin and neighbors while they instruct her in sexual conduct. When she has recovered, a large house is taken over by the women of the neighborhood, and men are expelled. Women of the locale visit, bringing gifts of food and beer, and then they dance, sing, drink, and feast for one or two days and nights. Some of the beer and food is also distributed to the men outside, who dance and enjoy themselves but who are excluded from the women's ceremonies inside. Sometimes a few men jokingly try to enter and are jostled and teased by the women who turn them back.

The initiate must demonstrate all she has been taught in the preceding days. Some of this differs from what is taught boys. Here are nine songs taught to both girls and boys but which particularly illustrate what Kaguru consider to be characteristics and problems peculiar to women:

1. "The milk of the goat flows from horn to horn!"

The semen received through sexual intercourse circulates through a girl's body, speeding the process of her maturation, here, the enlargement of her breasts and buttocks. Kaguru see sexual relations as contributing to a woman's fertility, hence, the belief that sexual relations after conception "feed" a pregnancy.

2. "I cut a piece from the *mugombi* tree! I cut a piece from the *musani* tree! We rub them together to see which is kindled!"

Two types of wood are used in kindling fire using traditional rubbing sticks. The hard piece is called male, the soft one which is kindled, female. To "make fire" with rubbing sticks is a common euphemism for sexual relations.

3. "The night belonged to the partridge! The cock made it his!"

This is said to mean that men master women in sexual relations. The symbolism here is very complex. The partridge is a wild, shy game bird of the bush, hunted by men. Its red feet are said to stand for menstruation—red, lowness. The cock is a proud and aggressive bird of the village; its red crest is associated with fire and fierceness.[1] Here, too, the cock is associated with the redness of dawn and the imposition of orderly day upon night, which is seen as dangerous and disorderly. Sexual mastery by men over women is important to Kaguru men because it is also associated with their notions of social and moral superiority.

4. "The fierce rhinoceros! It cruelly hurt me and mother!"

This is said to show that a girl has the same sexual experience as her mother, that there is a continuity between women of a lineage. The rhinoceros is a common motif for the wild, aggressive aspects of sexuality.

5. "It always rains rain, but the rain of February breaks the river banks."

This means that there is a periodic flow of blood with menstruation, but this is nothing compared to the blood lost at childbirth. Here, the symbolism of rain, moisture, and river valleys is used to produce an ambivalent tone. Rains are

---

[1] The reader should note that the destructive and warming qualities of fire are associated with women; but things may express many attributes, and here, fire is related to fierceness associated with men. Symbols are significant only within particular contexts.

desired by all Kaguru, but during the peak of the rainy season (February to March) the rains may wash away crops and cause as much harm as good.

6. "The bateleur eagles are in the sky, but they plunge down to cause crying!"

This means that a child does not cry in its mother's womb, but it does in her arms after it has been born. The bateleur eagle appears in some way to be associated with the ghosts of the dead who yearn to draw the child back and cause it to fret and cry. Birds in general are associated with omens and mystical signs, and the protecting ceremonies held when a newborn infant first emerges from the house of its birth are said to ward off predatory birds, especially bateleur eagles.

7. "The nose of the cow is moist year in and year out!"

Women are always polluting; this fact is expressed by a recurrent motif of moisture.

8. "The mouth of the wildcat is always open; let it be so, for it will never fill up."

This is said to mean that women are sexually voracious and insatiable. The preceding comments should make the symbolism clear.

9. "Wachikayanga! Help my children ford the river on your back! I cannot ford it with them for I have thorns on my back!"

Wachikayanga is a woman's name. The song is said to refer to all things a woman is prohibited from doing while she is menstruating. The usual word for menstruation is "sickness" (nhamu). A menstruating woman should not walk in gardens where there are crops, brew beer, prepare food, or come near people engaged in important tasks. In the past she was expected to sleep on the floor so as not to pollute her husband. In this song the woman cannot enter the stream for fear of polluting it. Kaguru say that there are proper spots in any river where only men or women should bathe, and that women should bathe at a spot downstream from men so as not to pollute them.

In the past a girl was usually married soon after her coming-out feast celebrating her arrival at womanhood. These celebrations still provide a good opportunity for a girl to survey the field of local eligible youths and for them, in turn, to see her charms. Today, now that more girls attend school, many do not marry for some years after initiation. A girl may have sexual activity even before initiation but should not conceive. It is said that in the past such an unwanted child would have been killed and the girl considered so shameless that she would probably be unmarriageable. Today (and perhaps even in the past) a pregnant but uninitiated girl would often simply have her initiation carried out hastily.

The songs and symbols of initiation may convey a somewhat distorted picture of Kaguru beliefs about themselves. It is true that women are considered less stable and responsible than men, but it is woman who, as epitomized by a mother, provides the ideal model for enduring sentiment and attachment. Women themselves, especially at initiation celebrations, sometimes joke and boast about their deceit of men and their need for many lovers. What are sometimes described as weaknesses are sources of boasting and mirth. Kaguru women certainly do not seem to consider themselves inferior to men and are deeply proud that they alone can carry on a lineage, yet much of Kaguru ritual and ceremonies asserts the moral and social superiority of men in many fields of activity. It may be that this is especially important for Kaguru men precisely because women are essential.

## Rites of Marriage

The rituals of marriage proceed according to somewhat different principles from those of initiation. Far more than in the case of initiation, these rituals express the problems created by the establishment of new sets of social relations which a Kaguru faces when entire groups, his and his spouse's, become joined through affinity. In the preceding chapters I discussed the reasons Kaguru give for marrying. Some involve the aims of individuals, but others relate to the establishment of ties between entire groups of people. These broader ties endure beyond the life span of the couple concerned. Kaguru marriage rites often tend to emphasize these continuous sides of marriage, especially as these are expressed in the birth of children which indissolubly link the two groups who become not merely affines but maternal and paternal kin to the same persons.

There are two important phases in a Kaguru marriage ceremony (*lusona*): (a) the formal exchange of bridewealth for the promise of a girl in marriage and (b) the actual cohabitation of the bride and groom when the marriage is consummated. Sometimes both these events take place on the same day, but the second may not follow until many weeks later. In the past payments were sometimes made over long periods, and cohabitation often took place years after the initial payments were made. In Christian marriages the payments precede the church wedding. The ceremony of payment is always at the village of the bride. The close kin of the groom along with the marriage go-betweens arrive at the girl's village. The bride and groom should be absent at such times, the bride remaining indoors and the groom, if he does come, remaining at a discrete distance from the actual transactions. Only men are allowed to be present. If women have come along, they go off and sit at a distance until the men's negotiations and payments are completed. The groom's father's kin open the payments, placing these in a container in front of the girl's father's kin. Then the groom's maternal kin make their payments in a container before the girl's maternal kin. The two kin groups should not mix their payments.

As various kinsmen contribute, each announces his particular contribution, implying future obligations for repayment and reciprocal help by his kin. The leaders on each side voices mock dissatisfaction (mock since the size of the payments has already been decided informally ahead of time through the marriage go-betweens). The offspring by which these two groups will be united will also be the source of competition for loyalties and favors, for Kaguru themselves are keenly aware of the future implications of any marriage they undertake. The act of social conjunction brings disjunction as well. At the marriage payment ceremony the two groups act out in a stylized, wryly funny preview the disputes which will color their future common relations.

*A Kaguru woman.*

Although today payments are usually in cash, they are still broken down into specially named payments which refer to various objects said to have been given in the past. For example, the girl's mother is given *mukowa* (carrying cloth) in payment for her having raised the girl; it is said that in the past this consisted of a female goat, but today it is usually cash. The girl's mother's brother is given *mulomo we kolo* (mouth of the lineage), and his acceptance signifies the lineage's agreement to the marriage; in the past this is said to have been a goat, but this too is now usually cash. *Mukiti* (closure) is given to the girl's kin where she resides in order to reserve the girl until the marriage is consummated; it is said that in the past this was required where negotiations and payments often took place long before the marriage was consummated and the suitor was keen to ensure that the girl would not be promised to someone else. Today the payment is still made even when all of the payments and the actual cohabitation take place on the same day. The definitive payment is called *chibanyo* and is said in the past to have been a chain necklace given to the bride's father. Many other similar terms are used in breaking down the payments; they call attention to the various obligations and ties between the girl and her kin. They indicate how payments are refracted along the different lines of kinship. This is even more important today than in the past, for now payments are usually in cash and thus not inherently different qualitatively, as are chains, hoes, cloth, male goats, female goats, and hens. When speaking about the size of a cash payment, a Kaguru will sometimes try to phrase it in terms of livestock, equating a certain unit of cash to a head of stock; by this he seeks to endow such payments with a dignity and substance which he feels is lacking in mere cash. These terms endow each cash subpayment with its only social and symbolic identity.

After all the payments have been made, the bride's father presents the group with a gourd of castor oil and proceeds to anoint several persons of the two groups of kin to be joined through the marriage. It is said that in the past only a girl from the bride's lineage and a boy from the groom's were anointed; today nearly everyone present who is kin to the couple may be anointed.

When the groom arrives at the bride's village to consummate the marriage, he is sometimes offered food and cash. He tastes the food and then returns both it and the cash, adding a bit to the latter. This is again returned with more food and cash added. He then takes the cash and eats the food. This again represents the many exchanges which will continue to take place not only while the couple are married but so long as their offspring live and future marriage payments continue to involve these groups.

On the day the marriage is consummated and the couple begin to cohabit, the bride's kin provide a large feast and much beer. There is dancing and drinking far into the night. All who come should bring some small gift of beer, food, or cash for the girl's kin, who are bearing all these expenses. At some marriages the couple is fed beans and dried meat to symbolize a happy marriage; the word beans (*kunde*) is a play on the word *kunda* (to love), and dried meat (*kang'ale*) is a play on *kakangala* (to endure difficulties). During much of this time the women will cry out, "*Cheleko! Cheleko!*" ("Birth! Birth!") because marriage is like birth since the couple sets out on a new life and since they will produce children.

Traditionally, the bride and groom should remain together at least four days and nights during the first period of cohabitation. They should not work and should have food brought to them by her kin. They are treated as children and are often told how to do simple tasks which they mastered long ago; they are like children growing up. The same term, *mwali* (novice, young person, youth, or maiden), is applied to them as is applied to newly initiated persons. The bride is supposed to report to a kinswoman, preferably a woman of a maternal grandmother status, on the sexual adequacy of her husband, and this is often a source of considerable anxiety to the husband. For this reason the initial days may be ones of much tension and effort for the youth. After the couple emerge from their confinement the bride's kin provide a small feast, *kwingisa* (entering), at which the groom eats with his new father-in-law. Until the birth of several children the groom must scrupulously avoid his mother-in-law, out of respect and shame. In the past a bride resided with her kin at least until the birth of her first child, but today this is rarely done. Kaguru explain that the girl's maternal kin should deliver the first child and that she would be afraid and uneasy toward her husband's kin, especially his maternal kinswomen, whose children would be in competition with hers for his inheritance. In the past her prolonged residence at home would also have been a way to enforce his rendering brideservice for her kin by helping them in garden work, herding, and house building.

An abbreviated kind of marriage ritual is performed to inherit the wife of a deceased maternal kinsman. In the past the woman was given beer which was then given to her choice among her deceased husband's assembled kin. Her husband's joking partners would officiate, mockingly bringing up all the past quarrels and enmities which had upset the group. They would also help cleanse the woman of her dead husband before she was allowed to cohabit with a new mate. Widowers were never ritually cleansed in this way unless they were polygynous and the pollution of one wife's death might be immediately transferred to another. Where the widower was monogamous, the period of mourning and the interim required to secure and pay for a new wife was thought sufficient to preclude contamination.

## Burial and Funeral Rites

For Kaguru a death presents two basic problems which, in part, at least, they attempt to deal with through ritual.[2] One problem involves the ways by which the dead person may be removed from the land of the living and safely transferred to the land of the ghosts. Death is comparable to any other change of status in which a person's relation to others must be redefined; here, one changes from a living person to an ancestral ghost. The problematical aspect of this transition involves the period when the person has just died but has not yet entered the land of the dead. At this point he is nearby the living and able to affect them easily, yet he cannot be controlled by the conventional ways which Kaguru use with their living comrades. Such "undead" are as dangerously undetermined as the young initiates who have been circumcised but not yet healed and are therefore neither adults nor children, neither part of the village nor the bush.

Kaguru believe there are good deaths and bad deaths. A bad death is one due to leprosy, dysentery, or being killed as punishment for witchcraft, recidivism, or for an inauspicious birth such as being born a twin or feet first. In the past the corpses of such persons were thrown into the bush. There was no point in burying them since they could not become proper ancestral ghosts; only proper human beings can enter the land of the ghosts. Instead, such persons are thought to wander about the bush causing harm to humans.

The dead person has assumed many of the supernatural powers of ghosts but is not responsive to the ordinary rites used to control the dead. Kaguru ritual attempts to move the deceased person out of the dangerous and difficult transitional phase and into a more responsive and tractable status. It also sets up as many

---

[2] I have discussed Kaguru funerals in some detail elsewhere (Beidelman 1966).

barriers and controls as possible in order to prevent any disruptive contact between this dangerous "unperson" and the living.

Joking partners perform the actual chores of burial. A person who died an ordinary death is washed by his joking partners, shaved all over, and then wrapped in a plain black or white cloth. Men are buried unclothed and on their right sides; women with a small pubic apron and on their left sides. In both cases the bodies are oriented with their feet toward the east and heads to the west, the direction of the land of the ghosts. For coming into contact with such dangerous pollution joking partners are given some cash and perhaps some of the dead person's clothing. All of the dead's clothing must be washed, and a woman's cooking pots must be destroyed. Using a bit of thatch from the roof of the dead person's house, the joking partners asperse water over the house and everything within it in order to cleanse it of death.

The other problem posed by death involves the ways by which those who survive the deceased may reorganize their lives, especially as these involve the new distribution of property and statuses inherited from the dead person. Although these rites of inheritance at funerals mainly involve the living rather than the dead, the sentiments and ties between the living and the deceased are frequently used symbolically to reinforce the acceptance of these new patterns.

No one in a settlement should work on the day of a death. The kin of the dead should observe these restrictions for at least four days. The women should remain indoors, while the men should sit outside day and night. No one should have sexual relations or groom or dress themselves attractively. Whenever kin and friends arrive to express their condolences and concern, the women begin to wail inside, and the men outside explain the events surrounding the death. Children are prevented from seeing the corpse. It is referred to as the "elephant," and elders tell children that the deceased person was devoured by a monster. On the day formal mourning ends the mourners shave their hair and prepare for a funeral feast which marks the resumption of normal social life and the fixing of the deceased in the land of the ghosts. Few of the funeral and mourning rites involve the actual corpse; this is considered so polluting and dangerous that it is buried nearly immediately.

The most important set of death rites are held at the end of mourning when the final funeral provides the settlement of the deceased's estate, the final verdict on the causes of the death, and the responsibility for it—if any of the dead person's kin were thought derelict in their obligations to care for the deceased. When these matters are settled, the dead person is said to have been "forgotten" in the sense that he or she is now no longer in any sense among the living. The deceased's joking partners and his paternal kin are the major speakers at such affairs. These two groups are thought to be least biased in commenting upon the affairs of the matrilineage. Kaguru sometimes quip that the main topic at death is marriage. By this they mean that the main issue of discussion and dispute over a dead person's estate involves wealth accumulated through previous marriage payments and how this should be transmitted to the heirs who are owed previous obligations. If a dead man held an important position of leadership which would be inherited, his heir is given his bow as a symbol of the authority and rights he is receiving; a girl might be given her mother's cosmetic oil gourd and jewelry. For Kaguru burial is a relatively simple rite; it is the funeral that involves many complaints and complexities and much tension and time.

These final services are sometimes held many weeks to as much as a year after the burial. In part this is because a large supply of food and beer is required to feed all who attend; more important, a final settlement requires that all of the close kin of the deceased attend and that a final agreement on inheritance be reached. This sometimes requires many preliminary preparations and much discussion.

With the rituals of death, the Kaguru complete a circle of personal development. Although Kaguru do not believe in transmigration of souls in the narrow sense we mean by the term, it is clear that the vitality of the ghosts is thought by them to be related to fertility, that the newborn emerge in some way from the land of the ghosts and the living return there. In a sense Kaguru rituals mark the round of existence, life-death-life; without the tags and forms provided by symbols these profound and powerful changes could neither be understood nor harnessed by Kaguru to provide some kind of social continuity and order.

# 8

# The Christian Mission:
# An Alien Institution Transplanted

K AGURU INSTITUTIONS which are essentially traditional have been described in the preceding chapters, although some of these institutions have been profoundly altered by modern, alien factors. I tried to show some overall patterns in these beliefs and activities. In this chapter, by way of contrast, I discuss an alien institution, a Christian mission, in order to show how it has been affected by being transplanted abroad. In part this is because the general features of Kaguru society affect any institution acted out by Kaguru even when this involves an alien set of values and practices not consistent with the traditional forms of Kaguru culture. Far more important, however, the general problems of colonial rule anywhere lead to the difficulties in communication and exercise of power which were discussed in Chapter 6. The Christian mission is (or was) an essentially colonial institution, and it too reflects social aspects of colonialism. Consequently, the Christian mission could no more resemble its mother church than the colonial government could resemble the parent government back in Europe. The missionary church took its peculiar form because it was imposed through the medium of a colonial situation, and because it was dominated at the higher, decision-making levels by Europeans (and later Australians) who sought to impose their goals and values upon an African population which did not accept many of these alien concepts.

## The Missionary Ethos and the Early Mission

In the nineteenth century many European Christian churches sent missionaries to Africa. These missionaries believed in the obligation of the church to convert all unbelievers to the faith. It is difficult to separate these spiritual goals from economic and political ones. At times European governments encouraged missionaries as the unofficial forerunners to colonization. These religious groups made the assumption that Christianity was inextricably linked with other aspects of European culture and values. It was assumed that only Christianity was the appropriate moral system for modern economic practices and government. Liter-

*Kaguru leaving C.M.S. Church*

acy, modern technology, modern medicine, and Christianity were presented to Africans as all of one piece even though this same Victorian era saw serious conflicts between the worlds of the scientists and intellectuals and the religious establishment.

When colonial administrators sought African clerks and skilled laborers, they looked to the missions. It was thought that Christian values would make Africans more willing to accept rule by Europeans. Initially, administrators hoped to secure educational services from the missions without any investment themselves; later the government paid annual subsidies to various missions in order to encourage their educational work. In the early colonial period different missionary groups ran into bitter conflict with one another over which would work in each area. Sometimes Christians destroyed one another's outposts and even harmed one another's converts. To end what they considered a misapplication of zealous energy, the German and later the British colonial governments established missionary spheres of influence. In each of these only one missionary group might operate legally. Only the towns and a few highly populated areas were excluded from this restriction. All of Kaguruland was affected, being given over exclusively to the Church Missionary Society, a branch of the Church of England.

During its formative years the C.M.S. (the common abbreviation for the Church Missionary Society) in East Africa was staffed mainly by British. With the economic depression of the 1930s, the British branch of the society found it difficult to meet its financial obligations; to relieve these difficulties the East African area, including Kaguruland, was transferred to the society's Australian branch. This influenced the direction subsequently taken by the mission and the attitude of many Kaguru toward it. The Australian branch of the Anglican church tended to emphasize the more pentecostal or fundamentalistic aspects of the church and took a strict and puritanical view of personal morality. Revivalism was encouraged, and alcohol, tobacco, gambling, and dancing were forbidden. Political activism, anticolonial sentiments, and interest in commerce by Africans were all seen as questionable activities likely to lead to worldly, unchristian behavior.

One of the most serious difficulties of the mission in the years since national independence has been its need to efface its earlier image among many Kaguru as a dour, intolerant, and semiofficial arm of the now-defunct colonial regime. Yet this is not to minimize the benefits which early missionaries brought to many Kaguru. The first and for many years the only medical services in the area were provided by the missionaries, and what education Kaguru received was in large part due to the efforts of the church.

## The Formal Structure of a Missionary Church

In the colonial period, the C.M.S. in Kaguruland was subordinate to a bishop residing more than a hundred miles to the west and to various technical supervisors and administrators also often residing elsewhere. All of these were Europeans, usually Australians.[1] The center of missionary activities in Kaguruland was the station of Berega, located about 8 miles from the Native Authority headquarters at Mamboya. All of the European missionaries in Kaguruland resided there. This was also the site of a small hospital and clinic with a doctor and several nurses, a primary school (grades 1–4), a "middle" school (grades 5–8), a mission-run general store, and a church. Some land was alienated to the mission and used for gardens cultivated by the students at the schools and by local mission employees. The station was surrounded by clusters of Kaguru settlements. Besides this site, the mission also controlled over a dozen primary schools in outlying areas of Kaguruland, as well as many small churches. Each school was provided with several houses of better than average standards (metal roofs and cement floors and walls) for the teaching staff.

Most of the activities of the mission may be divided into three broad spheres: medical work, confined to the Berega station; educational services run through the government-subsidized schools throughout the chiefdom; and purely religious services. Local church committees meet annually to determine policies for all these activities, but, in fact, these are generally run by those mission members continuously involved in these affairs from day to day. Most of the African members of the local committees lack the education and information to make their views effective with the missionary and government elite who actually control such policies.

## Medical Services and the Mission

Even today the only medical doctor to reside in Kaguruland is a missionary. The government has a doctor at the administrative headquarters 60 miles to the

---

[1] I follow the East African practice of terming all white persons "Europeans." In most situations, Africans saw little reason for making finer distinctions (though they were aware of them) since vis-à-vis Africans most white persons behaved roughly the same.

south and operates several clinics under medical aids, but locally any urgent illness and surgery must be dealt with through the mission. The staff of the mission clinic work at low salaries, far lower than those of government officers; yet lack of mission funds leads them to charge Africans small fees for services and medicines. In contrast, government medical services are usually free. Kaguru insist that the government does not expand its medical services to their area because the mission is already there, though to judge from the lack of medical services in bush areas elsewhere in the country, this seems a poor argument.

The mission's medical services provide a means of contact with non-Christians. A prayer service is held every morning before medical work begins, and all patients should take part, if only passively. The members of the clinic try to associate medical skill and aid with Christianity; sometimes this line of proselytization succeeds. Ironically, the genuine altruism of the mission staff is not usually seen as especially laudatory by local Africans since they have paid for such services. To the Africans this creates a contractual arrangement. Few Kaguru believe that the medical services operate at a loss.

The poverty of the European missionaries has many disadvantages in their work. The general life style of Europeans in East Africa is to avoid accepting cash or gifts from Africans but to provide them with occasional gifts. Europeans are accustomed to give extra food, old clothing, and other goods to African employees or their kin. In contrast, the missionaries' poverty leads them to be concerned with money so that they sometimes charge for small items in situations in which other Europeans would often simply give these away in a grand manner. Missionaries sometimes insist that Africans pay gasoline money to be transported in a mission vehicle, something a European government official or planter would never do. Such actions serve to reinforce the Kaguru stereotype of the missionary as less than the individual he claims to be. In any case, the poverty of the missionary is poverty only by contrast to his fellow Europeans in the colony; Kaguru contrast the missionary's auto, clothing, and house (simple, indeed, by European standards) with their own poverty and find it difficult to accept the missionary's frequent protests of self-sacrifice for his beliefs. Christian sermons are not sufficient to counteract profound differences in cultural definitions of poverty and equality.

The medical missionaries have trained some local African nurses. Clinics employ as many as a dozen other local people in associated menial tasks. Since patients' kin must buy or bring food for resident patients, the clinic brings a very large number of people into the area, providing indirect sources of income for local people.

## The Educational Services

Education is unquestionably the most important aspect of mission affairs; it involves the largest staff, the grestest finance, and the most important means of access to local Africans. To put matters crudely, by having a near monopoly on education in Kaguruland, the mission hopes that all influential and able young Kaguru may be indoctrinated into the Protestant faith. In the past mission schools, being subsidized by public funds from a United Nations Trusteeship, were technically open to children of every religious persuasion; in practice considerable pressure was put upon any student in attendance to accept the doctrine of the mission. Religious instruction was mandatory at all levels.

The past dependence of the mission upon the government for subsidies encouraged a more conservative political attitude there than that held by some of the richer missions such as some of the Roman Catholic groups, the staffs of which were usually of nationalities other than British. Political activity by mission employees was strongly discouraged. There were a few government-run schools in Kaguruland, but the establishment of each had been sharply criticized and opposed by the mission.

Although the government paid the greater part of the costs of education in all schools, Kaguru were required to pay school fees and other costs at a higher rate at mission schools than at government schools. Naturally, some Kaguru agitated for government schools to replace those run at greater charge.

The past monopoly of the mission in education led to very wide control over its employees. Government-employed teachers were discouraged from politics, but otherwise they had considerable freedom in their private lives. In contrast, mission teachers were required to lead exemplary "Christian" lives, refraining from adultery, alcohol, dancing, and smoking (at least in any open manner). Teachers who failed to conform were often dismissed, a severe punishment since the government usually refused to hire a teacher who had a bad recommendation from the mission. These teachers often found themselves unable to find alternate employment locally at jobs and salaries up to their expectations. The mission also encouraged its staff to attend church and to contribute part of their salaries as tithes. In return the teachers were the best-paid Africans in the chiefdom their salaries ranging from 250–500 shillings ($35–75) per month, and they were given cheap housing and access to garden land held by the mission. The general prestige of a teacher and his freedom, due to his education, from local traditional political pressures, meant an enviable life. Although teachers formed an economic elite, they were unable to invest money openly in any manner which might increase their wealth. The obvious mode of capital investment in Kaguruland was petty shopkeeping or brewing. The mission frowned on its staff engaging in any side business; however, some elderly mission employees circumvented this disapproval by setting up their grown children in business. This was often important to mission teachers since they were not eligible for pensions such as those provided for government teachers.

Why then did educated Kaguru stay with the mission, despite their dissatisfaction with conditions? Two reasons stand out: (a) The intensive and daily education along Christian lines had its effect, and despite their complaints, most Kaguru teachers firmly believed in Christianity. Some cited Christian principles in phrasing their complaints against the European missionaries. (b) Many Kaguru dislike leaving their homeland. Almost every Kaguru who was educated and tried to remain in Kaguruland had no choice but to seek employment with the mission, and having done so, the mission's relation with government educational administrators prevented him from leaving the system later. Few educated Kaguru could be found in the chiefdom who were not controlled economically and ideologically by either the mission or the government. In the colonial era African nationalism was covertly supported by many of these men, but its active organization came from outside Kaguruland, from the towns and estates where men of education, administrative skill, and social sophistication could find employment, security, and anonymity and thus be relatively free from direct and all-inclusive controls by Europeans.

## Religious Services

In Kaguruland, all European missionaries have religious interests, but only a few are actually ordained ministers. However, even among these groups there are everyday tasks of another order such as medical work, administration of finance, or supervision of schools. When I was in Kaguruland, there were several African pastors one of whom, an archdeacon, formally outranked any local European pastors. However, he was unable to read or speak English and, although exceedingly energetic and intelligent, was unable to gain access to the information (mostly in English) essential to policy decisions. He was consulted by European missionaries regarding local conditions, especially local persons and their affairs, but at no time was he placed in any position in which he might formally and openly appear to control or order Europeans. Yet the archdeacon had considerable power in the area, mainly for reasons similar to those providing power to Kaguru headmen and chiefs. The European missionaries had virtually no contact with Africans outside the narrow confines of the mission station. The C.M.S. followed a policy of circulating its staff from station to station so that while all missionaries knew Swahili, none knew the Kaguru language. The archdeacon, and to a lesser extent other pastors and leaders, had important ties with the wider community. The archdeacon married off kin to many other prominent local political and mission leaders in the area. He thereby stood, as did those in the Native Authority, between the colonial Europeans and the local population. He reported local moral lapses to the mission and provided information on how European policies might be effected. With shrewdness he could use this pivotal position to augment his influence.

Unlike teachers, clerks, or other technical staff, local Kaguru ministers have relatively little formal education. In contrast to the Roman Catholic Church, the C.M.S. places a fairly low premium upon formal requirements for conversion and sophisticated religious instruction for clerics. Consequently, pastors have relatively little prestige based on modern criteria and few means of using their pastoral skills on a broader social basis, as would be possible were they better educated and better paid. Their salaries compare to those of the members of the Native Authority; consequently, they engage in farming to survive. Kaguru pastors are meant to oppose the old social order with a new, but they are denied the most powerful advantages in that new order. The low economic status of pastors discourages abler, educated younger Kaguru from entering the clergy so that today it tends to be a status associated with the older generation.

If pastors have local power, it lies in nonreligious ties to kin and neighbors. The influence of the African archdeacon was an exception to this generalization because of his unusual position of continuous daily access to the Europeans (since he resided at Berega), his covert business enterprises, and his exceptional personal character. Pastoral assistants, catechists, and evangelists have less status than pastors and are not regularly paid in most cases. At best they receive occasional payments to cover their expenses while teaching or preaching. The mission is cautious about providing recognition to persons whose training is scant and who work so far from Europeans that they cannot be easily supervised. Mission activities provide prestige and recognition mainly in nonreligious spheres; local Africans remarked on the apparent inconsistency of such a situation, which is the result of a perpetual lack of funds and a religious ideology which emphasizes spontaneous, confessional faith and zeal rather than more formalistic, sophisticated belief.

Although the mission has been in Kaguruland for over eighty years, its rate of conversion is not impressive, and even its building installations seem shabby by comparison to those of nearby competing missionary groups. It is difficult to determine whom to count as a Christian, for many who claim to be Christians never attend church, contribute nothing to mission costs, and smoke, dance, and drink. A few Kaguru who reported themselves as Christians to the government census takers also reported themselves as polygynists.

No more than 25 percent of Kaguru are even nominal Christians, and probably only about 15 percent are active Christian members of the church. In some areas, such as near the mission station at Berega about 70 percent claim to be Christians in some sense, but in areas more distant from mission influence as few as 3 percent are converted.[2]

One of the problems for the mission has been how to retain sufficient educated staff members who conform to mission morality. This is difficult because the only ready sanction open to the mission for punishing immorality is expulsion. Here is an example:

Alfredi was a teacher at a mission primary school. He taught for over five years with the mission and attended church regularly. He frequented the local beer clubs and was a notorious philanderer. However, he paid little attention to the local gossip about himself. His unfaithfulness was not openly criticized by his wife since he supported her and her children in a comfortable manner, and she feared he might lose his job if his infidelities became an official issue. He tended to make fun of and show disrespect toward some of his superiors within the mission. In 1958 he began an affair with a married woman living near the mission station. This woman was also having an affair with a local Native Authority leader who was an affine of one of the African mission leaders. It is rumored that this official complained vigorously concerning this. In 1959 Alfredi was dismissed due to his unseemly fornication and drinking. He is now employed as a clerk by an Arab in another part of the chiefdom. His new post provides him with less than half the pay he received from the mission.

There are a limited number of persons available for skilled work so that the mission can ill afford to dismiss too many backsliders. However, there is a way

---

[2] Unlike many other areas of Tanzania, especially the coast, very few Kaguru have become Muslims. Kaguru say that this is because they associate Islam with Arabs and the earlier slave trade.

in which sinners may be reabsorbed into the system without the church losing face and, in a way, even strengthening its values. This is through revivalism. The mission has always exhibited a pentecostal, revivalistic impulse, which appears to have intensified during the depression of the 1930s. It may even be that this was found to be a useful means to easy conversion when lack of funds discouraged more routinized, undramatic means requiring more time and labor. By publicly confessing one's sins, one can reinstate oneself with the mission. A "saved" person might even name other kin and neighbors as well when he confesses. Some of the revival meetings are quite dramatic, leading one Kaguru wit to term them the church's version of the cinema. Here are two examples:

Mateya was a primary school teacher. He had a love affair with a local woman, and this came to the attention of his superiors. He was dismissed. After a few months he confessed his sins publicly at a revival meeting and he was taken back as a schoolteacher. However, he was not allowed to teach in Kaguruland but was given a post in another district.

Luke was a teacher employed at a school in Kaguruland. He attracted much attention by his heavy drinking. He also slept with many local women whom he met at beer clubs. Eventually, he was transferred to another mission station 300 miles away. After two years there, he completely recovered from drinking and announced at a revival meeting that he was "saved." He was allowed to return as a teacher in Kaguruland.

Even the strongest Christian could not defy all tradition. Kaguru Christians who insist on a church wedding and condemn drinking and dancing usually give in to their pagan kin and allow celebrations back in their villages to please everyone. Kaguru desperately need kin and neighbors. Dependence on others is too important for a Kaguru to risk ignoring them, whatever his religious beliefs. Here is an example:

Anna was the wife of Senyagwa and was "saved" at a revival meeting. She began to criticize Senyagwa for his pagan beliefs and encouraged her children to do the same. Senyagwa did not divorce Anna but simply took a second, younger wife. Senyagwa was a very prominent and influential Kaguru and for many years was a subchief. Despite this, his first wife and children refused to associate with him and moved from Senyagwa's home to Berega. Shortly after being saved, Anna secured a job at the mission station at Berega, where she worked at the clinic. This prevented her from doing housework so she hired Maria, a local girl, to cook. Her eldest son Julius, had completed secondary school (partly through his father's help) and secured a clerical post in the capital, Dar es Salaam. Anna remained at Berega with her younger son, Nahum, and her daughter Yudia. Later Yudia went to Dar es Salaam to visit Julius and there she became pregnant by one of his friends. When she returned with this news, Anna told her that she was no decent Christian and refused to help her. Yudia sought aid from her father, Senyagwa, who reminded her of her previous conduct and refused to help.

Meanwhile, Julius became secretary of a local quasi-political group lead by some of the politically conscious young Kaguru who up to now had been frustrated in their attempts to organize any new kind of political movement to aid modernization. Soon Julius became reconciled with his father, apparently to secure his aid and blessing in this political movement.

Nahum, the younger son, took advantage of Maria his mother's housekeeper, and she became pregnant. He also sought reconciliation with Senyagwa in order to secure bridewealth to marry Maria.

In the midst of all these difficulties, Anna became seriously ill and lost her job at the mission. She did not improve in health at the mission clinic and left Berega to live halfway between Senyagwa's home and Berega. She was rumored to favor a reconciliation with Senyagwa, despite his persistent paganism and the second wife. Her kin sent her to the government hospital at the provincial capital, over 100 miles away, in an Arab truck for a fare of 300 shillings. Although she and her children set out as militant saved Christians, they are now without funds and very mellowed in their religious tolerance.

## Recent Developments

With independence the government has increased its controls over the mission's educational service and has prevented the mission from using its powers to enforce conformity in teachers who are now on a par with other teachers elsewhere. The ties between the mission and the government are weakened. It is no longer a situation involving the mere word between two sets of Europeans "keeping up face" against an African majority whom they rule. More opportunities exist locally for advancement outside the mission now that nearly all Europeans have left the area. The past ethos of the need for European administration at the higher levels is now a decided embarrassment to the missionaries when they view a land ruled by Africans at all levels. Belatedly, the mission now seems anxious to Africanize its staff, although it cannot pay salaries or offer prestigious posts to men of the educational caliber it requires. The C.M.S. religious monopoly over the area has ended, and Roman Catholics have begun work on the eastern edge of the chiefdom a project for which they had petitioned for decades prior to national independence. The Protestant church will undoubtedly remain in Kaguruland, but it is unlikely that it will remain a typical missionary church much longer. As African pride and sense of independence grow, the church must be Africanized or fade away; and as Kaguru take over higher posts, the old dichotomy of European and African values will no longer obstruct communication within the church group. Only when free exchange between members is possible can there be any approach toward the ideal of Christian equality which was one of the qualities which appealed to the first African converts before the colonial period got underway.

## Conclusions: A Mission as a Social Type

The mission is a passing phase in Kaguru society, a facet of the colonial experience, and many of its features do not differ appreciably from other aspects of colonial rule. Educational and medical facilities would have been introduced as part of the colonial process even if the area had not been missionized. This is not to minimize the efforts of the missionaries but simply to indicate that we should not look for any social features peculiar to the mission itself in these two spheres.

Certain aspects of mission activities make sense only in terms of the particular kind of mission this was, that is, its ideology and the social and ethnic background of its members. These issues are too complex to be discussed fully here, but a few general comments may suggest questions and lines of analysis. There have been considerable differences between missions staffed by people of the same nationality as the colonizing power and those of different national groups. For example, the C.M.S. was always staffed by members of the British Commonwealth recognizing the king or queen and the Archbishop of Canterbury as their ultimate leaders. This led to an anticolonial position by the C.M.S. during the period of German colonial rule, and to a very sympathetic position during the subsequent period of British mandate. Certainly, the C.M.S. held a far different attitude toward British colonial rule than, say, that held by Irish Catholic or American Lutheran missionaries elsewhere in the territory.

Protestantism has in general fostered a far different type of convert than Catholicism. Protestantism, especially that fundamentalistic, "low church" version held by Australians, places weight on zeal and requires less sophisticated mastery of church teachings than, for example, Catholicism. This is especially true when contrasting clergy; all African Catholic priests have the equivalent of a college education, while many African Protestant ministers such as those in Kaguruland have only a grade-school education. Also, the financial resources of the missions vary greatly; the international nature of Catholicism and the wealth of some American Protestant sects contrast with a lack of resources by some other groups such as this branch of the C.M.S.

Some sides of the church's dogma affects Kaguru social relations far more than some others. The church forbids divorce and polygyny. That this leads to difficulties in Kaguru society should be clear from the preceding discussion of matrilineality. Other positions by the church, such as its hostility to drink, tobacco, gambling, and dancing, are products of the background of the missionaries in the sense that not all branches of the Church of England take such a puritanical view of pleasure. Since drinking and dancing are essential to Kaguru *rites de passage*, this poses serious difficulties for many Kaguru Christians and their kin. Many Kaguru customs are not inherently at odds with Christianity but are, nonetheless, condemned as savage and wrong by missionaries. For example, many would regard the sexual instruction provided at initiation as a useful custom, one we are only now appreciating in many Western nations. The missionaries condemn this instruction as licentious and attempt to discourage church members from allowing their children to perform such rites. The mission has felt less than enthusiastic about many other Kaguru customs, such as "cousin marriage" and matrilineality, though they have found it difficult to explain to educated Kaguru why then the queen married her cousin Prince Philip.

The early missionaries were profoundly interested in African languages and customs and sought to record as much of these as possible, but when I was in Kaguruland, missionaries were almost totally uninterested and uninformed about local customs, language, and social organization. Although they strongly advocate certain moral stands, such as lowering bridewealth or requiring circumcision in a clinic (by a female doctor, at one point) rather than in bush camps, they are unable to indicate clearly any of the implications which these policies might have toward changing Kaguru values and social relations in other areas of social life. Without understanding the structure of a society, one cannot change it intelligently, even assuming that it should be changed.

Christianity, as presented by the mission, can only work within a small, insulated group in which most social factors are fairly well controlled by the mission, such as at the main mission station itself. So long as many Kaguru pagans as well as Christians share kinship and neighborhoods, this new code could never be followed entirely by any Kaguru. Kaguru cannot manage long without their kin and neighbors, and they cannot make a place for themselves in the modern independent African state without absorbing modern economic and political techniques.

In the colonial period the mission took little positive notice of Kaguru traditional life, even though this permeated all aspects of everyday Kaguru affairs, but, more seriously, it often described economic and political ambition by Africans as worldly and selfish. Neither of these two spheres of social life, the traditional nor the modern, was fully appreciated by the missionaries who claimed the moral authority to help Kaguru in their present circumstances and to lead them into a better future.

# 9

# Postscript

T HIS STUDY presents a society from two perspectives in time. It describes Kaguru society as it existed during the recent colonial period, and it also provides a sketch of some of the features of Kaguru society at an earlier period. Today the colonial picture I encountered during most of my fieldwork is outdated. Just as we had to take into account the precolonial situation in order to understand the colonial period, so too the colonial past provides a key to understanding current affairs in Kaguruland as part of a new and independent African state. What was previously the United Nations Trust Territory of Tanganyika (in practice, however, a British colony) is now the independent Republic of Tanzania. Nearly all Europeans have left Kilosa District, and the government is completely controlled by Africans themselves. Whereas earlier the European elite with authority were committed to a capitalistic oriented, nonegalitarian society, the present leaders of the country are attempting to promote a more socialistic, egalitarian regime. The Native Authority has been dissolved, and talk of tribalism or inherited office or rights is frowned upon. Many Indian and Arab shops which at one time seemed essential to the local economy have now gone out of business since the government has forbidden purchase by private traders of many local crops which now may be sold only to governmental agencies. Local courts are now run by African magistrates, mostly men from outside Kaguruland.

The area has altered greatly in terms of the formal political structure, the modes of marketing and distributing goods, and the agencies accelerating social change. Where courts meet less frequently and have judges unfamiliar with local customs, Kaguru now sometimes settle cases informally out of court, as in the traditional past. Where prices are not considered favorable for the sale of crops to government-sponsored buyers, black marketeering is carried out. These new measures for courts and marketing were planned to provide the ordinary people with a greater share in the government and to eliminate profit-making entrepreneurs between the small producers and the large exporters and consumers in the cities.

However, it takes more than a pronouncement on paper to undo generations of unequal education, training, and deployment of resources. Plans formulated on a national basis sometimes neglect the peculiar difficulties of particular areas. The poverty and illiteracy of the great majority of people in Kaguruland still mean that policies must be made and executed by a small minority with the education to plan and carry out complex, large-scale programs. Unfortunately, the policies have not always been successful. Minority decisions sometimes lead to resented rules which seem unfair or incomprehensible from below, and the temptation of corruption by an elite is always present in a poor country where even the elite may feel underpaid. Despite these difficulties, however, Tanzania as a whole remains one of those few nations in which a large number of its leaders continue to demonstrate essentially altruistic, sincere efforts to improve the general welfare of the land and to discourage forms of modernization likely to exploit the welfare of the many for the advantage of a few. The failures I mention are in large part the failures inevitable in any attempts to overcome a past of underdevelopment, undereducation, and neglect by alien rulers.

Customs die slowly, especially in a land of considerable poverty where illiteracy inhibits the spread of new ideas and practices. Marriages are still carried out as before; youths still fret about where to secure bridewealth and elders quarrel about its distribution. In the dry season one can still hear drumming celebrating circumcision and female initiation. Rainmakers are still sometimes consulted during droughts. If we read the early missionaries' accounts of the 1880s, we realize how profoundly many things have changed, and yet even in these old accounts there is much which reads familiarly today.

To discuss Kaguruland since African independence would require a second book, but the reader might well conjecture for himself what lines such development might take. What are the most fixed elements in Kaguru society, and what are those most responsive to change? How are these elements related to those factors which are most important in determining the form and quality of Kaguru society? Indeed, what are those factors?

Above all, whenever we read a description of a society, we should realize that we are reading an artificial construct necessary to understand something far more complex and mercurial than the model suggests. By the time we have analyzed a society and seen our work into print, much about that society may have already changed, even assuming that our analysis was somewhat accurate in the first place. Kaguru society of 1880, 1920, 1960, and 1970 is in each case something different, yet can we not speak of all these somehow as Kaguru society? If this book has been useful, it may suggest how one may go about answering some of these questions about what a society is and what artificial stereotypes we anthropologists and sociologists impose upon it whenever we presume to write about it. A reader may restudy Kaguruland, and such a study would be welcome. Like all societies, Kaguru society is too manifold to be explained by any one researcher, and a new fieldworker, building upon what has already been done, could hold up a different mirror to reflect some new view of the Kaguru way of life. Obviously, even the few facets presented here are open to different interpretations from those I have made. I hope that Africans will be among the students reading this study. If Africans are to build the new society they claim as their hope and right, they must first understand their history through constructing analytical models of their traditional societies and their colonial past. Their view is needed to write the future sociology which will complement (and at times correct) the work that has already been done mainly by aliens in their midst. If that work can tell us about the relation between social theory or models, on the one hand, and planned social change, on the other, then it will hold important lessons for those of us outside Africa as well.

# Glossary

I have tried to define terms only within the limited framework of how they are used in this text. A few terms such as "kinship" and "institution" are so complex as far as anthropology is concerned that I have avoided a definition here since a working understanding of these terms can be gained from the text itself.

AFFINE: A person to whom one is related through marriage. A crude English translation would be in-law.

*Akida:* African officials appointed by alien rulers (Arab, German, and British) to administer local African people, often not of the same ethnic group as the *akida.*

BANTU: A linguistic category which includes most of the language of the lower, southern half of Africa. The term comes from a root term for "people"; thus, the terms for "man" are similar in Kaguru *(munhu)*, Gogo *(munu)*, and Swahili *(mtu).*

BRIDEWEALTH: The wealth given by a groom and/or the group to which he is connected to various members of the bride's group in order to legitimize a marriage. This term is preferable to the term "brideprice" since the functions of this payment are far from those of a mere economic transaction. In any case, the bride is hardly "sold" to her husband's group since residual rights in her and her offspring remain with her kin, to whom she continues to be related.

CLAN: A group of persons who believe themselves linked through common descent, although they cannot trace each ancestor linking themselves to one another. In terms of the matrilineal Kaguru one may speak of a matriclan. The use of the term "clan" varies greatly among anthropologists.

DESCENT: The tracing of kinship relations back through time to common ancestors. This is the basic means of calculating kinship in most societies.

DIVINATION: The ability to gain knowledge about past, present, and future events and conditions by means of tapping supernatural powers aided by the use of various mechanical means such as casting objects on the ground and gazing into water. Fortune-telling through cards is a European form of divination.

ETHNOGRAPHY: The collection of descriptive facts about the way of life of a particular ethnic group. Social anthropology involves the interpretation of ethnographic data in terms of social theories.

EXOGAMY: The practice of marrying outside a particular social group. The converse of this is endogamy. Kaguru practice strict clan exogamy, having rules against intraclan marriages or sexual relations; they tend to be ethnically endogamous, but there are no rules against marrying outsiders, provided that if a Kaguru woman marries an alien, he must be a "proper" man (for Kaguru this means being circumcised).

INDIRECT RULE: The formal political policy carried out by the British in Africa whereby indigenous (or purportedly indigenous) political systems were utilized to govern colonially subject people through their own traditional systems of authority.

LINEAGE: A group of persons linked together through traceable descent to a common ancestor, reckoned exclusively through only one sex. The Kaguru reckon this through women. Membership in a lineage allocates important legal rights and obligations to persons and things in a society.

MAGIC: The manipulation of persons and things through the use of objects, words, and acts thought to give one access to supernatural powers for either good or evil purposes.

MATRILINEAGE: A lineage whose members are recruited by descent through women from a common ancestress. All the connections in these relations are traceable genealogically.

PATERNAL GROUP: The persons related to one through one's father; in a matrilineal system such as that of the Kaguru, this usually refers to a person's father's matrilineage.

PATRILINEAL: Referring to descent exclusively through men. Kaguru have certain patrilineal groups (called *mulongo*), but these cannot be termed proper lineages since no important rights or obligations are attached to them.

RITES DE PASSAGE: A term coined by the famous Belgian-French anthropologist Arnold van Gennep. It refers to the various rituals performed when a person passes from one important social status to another. The Christian sacraments are forms of *rites de passage.*

SHILLING: The East African shilling was the currency of the area at the time of research. There were one-hundred pennies in a shilling. Seven East African shillings equaled $1.00 U.S. currency.

SORCERY: The supernatural power to cause another person or that person's possessions harm through the use of various substances or acts. The efficacy of sorcery depends upon the nature of the acts performed rather than upon the moral character of the practitioner.

SWAHILI: The lingua franca of East Africa and much of the Congo. It is a composite of Bantu, Arabic, and European (Portuguese, English, and French) with a basic structure which conforms to other Bantu languages.

WITCHCRAFT: The power to exert supernatural harm upon another person or his possessions, that power depending upon inherent evil qualities in the evil person (witch) himself.

# References

BEIDELMAN, T. O., 1960, The Baraguyu. *Tanganyika Notes and Records,* 55:245–278.
————, 1961a, A Note on the Kamba of Kilosa District. *Tanganyika Notes and Records,* 57:181–194.
————, 1961b, Umwano und Ukaguru Students' Association. *Anthropos,* 56:818–845; republished in English translation in *Black Africa,* ed. J. Middleton. New York: Macmillan, 1970.
————, 1962, A History of Ukaguru, Kilosa District: 1857–1916. *Tanganyika Notes and Records,* 58 and 59:11–39.
————, 1963a, Kaguru Omens: An East African People's Concepts of the Unusual, Unnatural, and Supernormal. *Anthropological Quarterly,* 36:43–59.
————, 1963b, Five Kaguru Texts. *Anthropos,* 58:737–772.
————, 1964a, Intertribal Insult and Opprobrium in an East African Chiefdom (Ukaguru). *Anthropological Quarterly,* 37:33–52.
————, 1964b, Three Kaguru Tales of the Living and the Dead. *Journal of the Royal Anthropological Institute,* 94:109–137.
————, 1966, *Utani:* Some Kaguru Notions of Death, Sexuality, and Affinity. *Southwestern Journal of Anthropology,* 22:354–380.
————, 1967a, The Hehe of Ukaguru. *Afrika und Übersee,* 50:304–314.

————, 1967b, Intertribal Tensions in Some Local Government Courts in Colonial Tanganyika, part 1. *Journal of African Law*, 10:118–130.

————, 1968, Intertribal Tension in Some Local Government Courts in Colonial Tanganyika, part 2. *Journal of African Law*, 11:27–45.

————, 1970a, Some Sociological Implications of Culture, in *Theoretical Sociology*, eds. J. C. McKinney and E. Tiryakian. New York: Appleton. pp. 500–527.

————, 1970b, Myth, Legend, and Oral History: A Kaguru Traditional Text. *Anthropos* 65:74–97.

CAMERON, D., 1939, *My Tanganyika Service and Some Nigeria.* London: Allen & Unwin.

CHURCH MISSIONARY SOCIETY, 1901, *Proceedings of the C.M.S. for 1900–1901.* London: Church Missionary Society.

GREAT BRITAIN, 1927, *Report . . . on Tanganyika to the League of Nations . . . for 1926.* London: H. M. Stationery Office.

LEACH, E. R., 1954, *Political Systems of Highland Burma.* Cambridge, Mass.: Harvard University Press.

MAUSS, M., 1954, *The Gift [Essai sur le don, 1925].* New York: Free Press.

STANLEY, H. M., 1872, *How I Found Livingstone.* London: Sampson, Low.

————, 1899, *Through the Dark Continent.* London: G. Newnes.

# Further Readings

## General Cultural Area

BEIDELMAN, T. O., 1967, *The Matrilineal Peoples of Eastern Tanzania.* London: International African Institute.

————, 1969, Addenda to Bibliography of The Matrilineal Peoples of Eastern Tanzania. *Africa,* 39:186–187.

Surveys of the Kaguru and their matrilineal neighbors with full bibliographies.

## The Kaguru

BEIDELMAN, T. O., 1961a, Hyena and Rabbit: A Kaguru Representation of Matrilineal Relations. *Africa,* 31:61–74; reprinted in *Myth and Cosmos,* ed. J. Middleton. New York: American Museum of Natural History, 1967.

Use of a folktale to illustrate social relations.

————, 1961b, Beer Drinking and Cattle Theft in Ukaguru: Intertribal Relations in a Tanganyika Chiefdom. *American Anthropologist,* 54:534–549.

Discussion of the political and economic factors determining changing intertribal relations in Kaguruland.

————, 1961c, Kaguru Justice and the Concept of Legal Fictions. *Journal of African Law,* 5:5–20.

Discussion of some problems in interpreting legal concepts in an alien society.

————, 1961d, Right and Left Hand among the Kaguru: A Note on Symbolic Classification. *Africa,* 31:250–257.

An introduction to some key symbolic notions of the Kaguru.

————, 1963a, Further Adventures of Hyena and Rabbit: The Folktale as a Sociological Model. *Africa,* 33:54–69.

Use of a folktale to illustrate problems of authority in a matrilineal society.

————, 1963b, The Blood Covenant and the Concept of Blood in Ukaguru. *Africa,* 33:321–342.

An introduction to Kaguru notions about biological relations of kin.

———, 1963c, Kaguru Time Reckoning: An Aspect of the Cosmology of an East African People. Southwestern Journal of Anthropology, 19:9–20.

———, 1963d, "Witchcraft in Ukaguru," in *Witchcraft and Sorcery in East Africa*, eds. J. Middleton and E. H. Winter, pp. 55–98. London: Routledge & Kegan Paul Ltd.

## The Kaguru's Neighbors

BEIDELMAN, T. O., 1964, Pig *(Guluwe)*: An Essay on Ngulu Sexual Symbolism and Ceremony. *Southwestern Journal of Anthropology*, 20:359–392.

———, 1965, Notes on Boys' Initiation among the Ngulu. *Man*, 65:143–147.

These essays contain the fullest recent account of the Ngulu, the ethnic group most closely resembling the Kaguru.

RIGBY, P., 1966, Dual Symbolic Classification among the Gogo of Central Tanzania. *Africa*, 36:1–17.

———, 1968a, Some Gogo Rituals of "Purification," in *Dialectic in Practical Religion*, ed. E. R. Leach, Cambridge University Papers in Social Anthropology 5, pp. 153–178. London: Cambridge.

———, 1968b, Joking Relationships, Kin Categories, and Clanship among the Gogo. *Africa*, 38:133–155.

———, 1969, *Cattle and Kinship among the Gogo*. Ithaca, N.Y.: Cornell University Press.

These useful studies describe the Gogo who neighbor the Kaguru to the west.

YOUNG, R., and H. FOSBROOKE, 1960, *Smoke in the Hills*. Evanston, Ill.: Northwestern University Press.

A somewhat superficial study of the Luguru, a matrilineal society neighboring the Kaguru to the southeast.

## Matrilineal Systems

RICHARDS, A., 1956, *Chisungu*. London: Faber.

A pioneer study of female initiation among a matrilineal society, the Bemba of Zambia, Central Africa.

SCHNEIDER, D., and K. GOUGH, eds., 1961, *Matrilineal Kinship*. Berkeley, Calif.: University of California Press.

A general survey of some of the problems of matriliny. Useful data with much rich comparative material, although the introductory theoretical essay lacks insight.

TURNER, V. W., 1957, *Schism and Continuity*. Manchester: Manchester University Press.

———, 1968a, *The Forest of Symbols*. Ithaca, N.Y.: Cornell University Press.

———, 1968b, *Drums of Afflication*. Oxford: Clarendon Press.

Part of a detailed and excellent analysis of a matrilineal society, the Ndembu of Zambia, Central Africa.